FOURTH EDITION

ANTHOLOGY OF SCORES FOR

A History of Music in Western Culture

VOLUME ONE: Antiquity through the Baroque Era

FOURTH EDITION

ANTHOLOGY OF SCORES FOR

A History of Music in Western Culture

VOLUME ONE: Antiquity through the Baroque Era

Mark Evan Bonds

Department of Music
University of North Carolina at Chapel Hill

PEARSON

Boston Columbus Indianapolis New York San Francisco Upper Saddle River
Amsterdam Cape Town Dubai London Madrid Milan Munich Paris Montréal Toronto
Delhi Mexico City São Paulo Sydney Hong Kong Seoul Singapore Taipei Tokyo

President: *Yolanda de Rooy*
Editor-in-Chief: *Sarah Touborg*
Publisher: *Roth Wilkofsky*
Editorial Assistant: *Christopher Fegan*
VP Director of Marketing: *Brandy Dawson*
Executive Marketing Manager: *Kate Mitchell*
Marketing Assistant: *Paige Patunas*
Managing Editor: *Melissa Feimer*
Production Liaison: *Joe Scordato*
Full-Service Management: *GEX Publishing Services*

Production Editor: *GEX Publishing Services*
Senior Operations Specialist: *Diane Peirano*
Cover Score: *"Toccata IX," by Girolamo Frescobaldi, from IL SECONDO LIBRO DI TOCCATE, published in 1637.*
Composition: *GEX Publishing Services*
Printer/Binder: *R. R. Donnelley & Sons (Jefferson City)*
Cover Printer: *Lehigh-Phoenix Color (Hagerstown)*

This book was set in 9/11 Times Roman by GEX Publishing Services and was printed and bound by R. R. Donnelley & Sons. The cover was printed by Lehigh-Phoenix Color (Hagerstown).

Credits and acknowledgments borrowed from other sources and reproduced, with permission, in this textbook appear on pages 310–314.

10 9 8 7 6 5 4 3 2 1

ISBN 10: 0-205-92797-1
ISBN 13: 978-0-205-92797-5

CONTENTS

CREDITS

I Epitaph of Seikilos
(1st century C.E.)

((•−Listen
CD1   Track 1
mysearchlab (with scrolling translation)
Book p. 9

As long as you live, be happy;
do not grieve at all.
Life's span is short;
time exacts the final reckoning.

This brief piece, dating from the first century C.E., is in the Ionian *tonos,* occupying an octave on E that includes C♯ and F♯, with special prominence given to the pitch A. This last pitch, the middle note of the octave on E, constitutes the *mese* ("mean") of the range. "In all good music," comments the author of the *Problems* (possibly Aristotle), "*mese* occurs frequently, and all good composers have frequent recourse to *mese,* and, if they leave it, they soon return to it, as they do to no other note." Songs like this one are known to have been accompanied on the lyre or some similar instrument, but the accompaniment itself was never notated and remains a matter of considerable speculation.

Performance notes: Only the vocal line is notated, but this does not preclude the addition of instruments. Here, the lyra (lyre) plays the melody through once in its entirety before the vocalist sings her part with the lyra doubling the vocal line an octave below. The instrumentalist is playing the lyra with a plectrum, similar to a modern-day guitar pick.

2 Plainchant **Mass** for Christmas Day

((•−Listen
CD1   Track 2
mysearchlab (with scrolling translation)
Book p. 35

a) Introit (Propers)

Resurrexi, et adhuc tecum sum, alleluia:
posuisti super me manum tuam, alleluia:
mirabilis facta est scientia tua,
alleluia, alleluia.

Domine, probasti me, et cognovisti me:
tu cognovisti sessionem meam,
et resurrectionem meam.

Puer natus est nobis, et filius datus est nobis:
cuius imperium super humerum eius:
et vocabitur nomen eius, magni consilii Angelus.
et vocabitur nomen eius, magni consilii Angelus.

I arose and am still with thee, alleluia:
thou hast laid thy hand upon me, alleluia;
thy knowledge is become wonderful,
alleluia, alleluia.

Lord, thou hast proved me, and known me:
thou hast known my sitting down
and my rising up.

Unto us a Child is born, unto us a Son is given.
The government shall be upon His shoulder,
and His name shall be called Wonderful, the
Angel of Great Counsel.
V. Sing unto the Lord a new song, for He has
done wonderful things.

b) Kyrie (Ordinary)

Kyrie eleison.
Christe eleison.
Kyrie eleison.

Lord have mercy.
Christ have mercy.
Lord have mercy.

c) Gloria (Ordinary)

d) Gradual (Propers)

Gloria in excelsis Deo.
Et in terra pax hominibus bonae voluntatis.
Laudamus te. Benedicimus te.
Adoramus te. Glorificamus te.
Gratias agimus tibi propter magnam gloriam tuam.
Domine Deus, Rex caelestis.
Deus Pater omnipotens.
Domine Fili unigenite Jesu Christe.
Domine Deus, Agnus Dei, Filius Patris.
Qui tollis peccata mundi,
miserere nobis.
Qui tollis peccata mundi,
suscipe deprecationem nostram.
Qui sedes ad dexteram Patris,
miserere nobis.
Quoniam tu solus sanctus.
Tu solus Dominus.
Tu solus Altissimus, Jesu Christe.
Cum Sancto Spiritu,
in Gloria Dei Patris. Amen.

Glory to God in the highest.
And on earth peace to men of good will.
We praise thee, we bless thee,
we adore thee, we glorify thee.
We give thee thanks for thy great glory.
O Lord God, King of heaven,
God the Father almighty.
O Lord, the only begotten Son, Jesus Christ.
O Lord God, Lamb of God, Son of the Father.
Thou who takest away the sins of the world,
have mercy on us.
Thou who takest away the sins of the world,
receive our prayer.
Thou who sittest at the right hand of the Father,
have mercy on us.
For thou only art holy,
thou only art Lord,
thou only art most high, O Jesus Christ,
with the Holy Ghost,
in the glory of God the Father. Amen.

Viderunt omnes fines terrae
salutare Dei nostri:
jubilate Deo omnis terra.
Notum fecit Dominus salutare suum:
ante conspectum gentium revelavit
justitiam suam.

All the ends of the earth have seen
the salvation of God:
sing joyfully to God, all the earth.
The Lord hath made known his salvation:
before all nations he has revealed his
righteousness.

Listen

CD1 Track 4
mysearchlab (with scrolling translation)
Book p. 35

e) Alleluia (Propers)

Alleluia.
Dies sanctificatus illuxit nobis;
venite gentes et adorate Dominum,
quia hodie descendit lux super terram.

Alleluia.
A holy day has dawned for us;
come, ye nations, and praise the Lord,
for today a great light has desended to earth.

f) Credo (Ordinary)

Et i-te-rum ven-tu-rus est cum glo-ri-a ju-di-ca-re vi-vos

et mor-tu-os: cu-jus re-gni non e-rit fi-nis. Et in Spi-ri-tum San-ctum,

Do-mi-num, et vi-vi-fi-can-tem: qui ex Pa-tri-e Fi-li-o-que pro-ce-dit.

Qui cum Pa-tre et Fi-li-o si-mul ad-o-ra-tur et con-glo-ri-fi-ca-tur:

qui lo-cu-tus est per Pro-phe-tas. Et u-nam san-ctam ca-tho-li-cam

et a-po-sto-li-cam Ec-cle-si-am. Con-fi-te-or u-num ba-ptis-ma

in re-mis-si-o-nem pec-ca-to-rum. Et ex-spec-to re-sur-rec-ti-o-nem mor-tu-o-rum.

Et vi-tam ven-tu-ri-sae-cu-li. A-men.

Do-mi-nus vo-bis-cum. R. Et cum spi-ri-tu tu-o. O-re-mus.

Credo in unum Deum.	I believe in one God,
Patrem omnipotentem,	Father almighty,
factorem caeli et terrae,	maker of heaven and earth
visibilium omnium et invisibilium.	and of all things visible and invisible.
Et in unum Dominum Jesum Christum,	And in one Lord Jesus Christ,
Filium Dei unigenitum.	the only-begotten Son of God,
Et ex Patre natum.	born of the Father
ante omnia saecula.	before all ages.
Deum de Deo, lumen de lumine,	God of God, light of light,
Deum verum de Deo vero.	true God of true God.
Genitum, non factum,	Begotten, not made,
consubstantialem Patri:	being of one substance with the Father,
per quem omnia facta sunt.	by whom all things were made.

Qui propter nos homines et propter nostram salutem descendit de caelis.	Who for us men and for our salvation came down from heaven.
Et incarnatus est de Spiritu Sancto ex Maria Virgine:	And was made incarnate by the Holy Ghost of the Virgin Mary,
Et homo factus est.	and was made man.
Crucifixus etiam pro nobis:	And was crucified for us
sub Pontio Pilato passus et sepultus est.	under Pontius Pilate. He suffered and was buried
Et resurrexit tertia die,	And the third day he rose again
secundum Scripturas.	according to the Scriptures.
Et ascendit in caelum:	And ascended into heaven,
sedet ad dexteram Patris.	and sitteth on the right hand of the Father.
Et iterum venturus est cum gloria	And he shall come again with glory to judge
judicare vivos et mortuos:	the quick and the dead;
cujus regni non erit finis.	of whose kingdom there shall be no end.
Et in Spiritum Sanctum, Dominum,	And in the Holy Ghost,
et vivificantem:	Lord and giver of life,
qui ex Patrie Filioque procedit.	who proceedeth from the Father and the Son.
Qui cum Patre et Filio simul adoratur	Who, together with the Father and the Son,
et conglorificatur:	is worshiped and glorified;
qui locutus est per Prophetas.	who spake by the prophets.
Et unam sanctam catholicam	And one holy, Catholic,
et apostolicam Ecclesiam.	and Apostolic Church.
Confiteor unum baptisma	I acknowledge one baptism
in remissionem peccatorum.	for the remission of sins.
Et exspecto resurrectionem mortuorum.	And I look for the resurrection of the dead,
Et vitam venturi saeculi. Amen.	and the life of the world to come. Amen.
Dominus vobiscum.	The Lord be with you.
Et cum spiritu tuo.	And with thy spirit.
Oremus.	Let us pray.

g) Offertory (Propers)

((•—Listen
CD1   Track 5
mysearchlab (with scrolling translation)
Book p. 35

Offertory

4. Tu-i sunt * cae-li, et tu-a est ter-ra:

or-bem ter-ra-rum, et ple-ni-tu-di-nem e-jus

tu fun-da-sti: ju-sti-ti-a et ju-di-ci-um

prae-pa-ra-ti-o se-dis tu-ae.

Tui sunt caeli et tua est terra,	Thine are the heavens, and thine is the earth,
orbem terrarum et plenitudinem ejus tu fundasti.	The world and its fullness you have founded.
Justitia et judicium praeparatio sedis tuae.	Righteousness and justice are the basis of your throne.

h) Sanctus (Ordinary)

Sanctus, Sanctus, Sanctus	Holy, holy, holy,
Dominus, Deus Sabaoth.	Lord God of Hosts.
Pleni sunt caeli et terra gloria tua.	The heavens and earth are full of thy glory.
Hosanna in excelsis.	Hosanna in the highest.
Benidictus qui venit in nomine Domine.	Blessed is he who comes in the name of the Lord.
Hosanna in excelsis.	Hosanna in the highest.
Per omni a saecula saeculorum. Amen.	World without end. Amen.

i) Agnus Dei (Ordinary)

Agnus Dei,	Lamb of God,
qui tollis peccata mundi:	who takest away the sins of the world,
miserere nobis.	have mercy on us.
Agnus Dei,	Lamb of God,
qui tollis peccata mundi:	who takest away the sins of the world,
miserere nobis.	have mercy on us.
Agnus Dei,	Lamb of God,
qui tollis peccata mundi:	who takest away the sins of the world,
dona nobis pacem.	give us peace.

Listen

CD1   Track 6
mysearchlab (with scrolling translation)
Book p. 35

j) Communion (Propers)

Viderunt omnes fines terrae	All the ends of the earth have seen
salutare Dei nostri.	the salvation of God.

The sung portions of the Mass consist of elements whose texts are fixed and unchanging—the Ordinary—and elements whose texts vary according to the particular Sunday or feast day within the liturgical year—the Propers.

Ordinary: The Kyrie, Gloria, Credo, Sanctus, and Agnus Dei are the main elements of the Ordinary. (The *Pater noster*—the Lord's Prayer—and the concluding *Ite, missa est* are also unchanging but are recited in a formulaic fashion.) The Gloria and Credo, which have relatively long texts, are largely syllabic. The Kyrie, Sanctus, and Agnus Dei, all of which have relatively brief texts, are predominantly neumatic with a mixture of syllabic and mildly melismatic passages.

Propers: The Collect, Epistle, Gospel, Preface, and Post-Communion are of relatively little musical interest and are not included in the anthology here, as they are sung according to a formulaic pattern centering on a single recitation tone.

The Introit, Gradual, Alleluia, Sequence, Offertory, and Communion, on the other hand, are musically rich and varied, and they constitute the bulk of the chant repertory for the Mass. The Introit, Offertory, and Communion are sometimes called "action chants" because they accompany actions of the priest and his attendants who are celebrating Mass: the Introit is sung during the procession into the church, the Offertory during the presentation of the bread and wine, the Communion during the distribution of the bread and wine. These chants are typically built around a psalm verse. *Puer natus est nobis*, the Introit for the Mass on ChristmasDay, for example, incorporates a psalm verse (*Cantate Domino*) that is essentially recitational, centering on a single "recited" note (here, the pitch D). But the much longer introduction to the Psalm verse (*Cantate Domino . . . fecit*) is freely composed in terms of both its text and its music. The setting is neumatic, with melismas of four and five notes distributed liberally throughout. The Offertory and Communion for Christmas Day are even more elaborate, with long melismas in both.

The most elaborate chants in the Mass are the Gradual and Alleluia, both of which feature relatively brief texts. The Alleluia repertory in particular is known for its florid, exuberant melodies, especially on the final syllable of the word *alleluia,* a passage known as the *jubilus* (derived from the same root word as the word "jubilation"). The Gradual and Alleluia are called responsorial chants because the chorus alternates with ("responds to") the soloist or a small group of soloists. In the Gradual for Christmas Day, *Viderunt omnes*, the soloist intones the opening two words (up to the asterisk marked in the score), at which point the chorus enters (*finis terrae . . .*). (Modern performances, including the one here, rarely observe this distinction between soloist and chorus in the intonation.) This entire unit is known as the respond (refrain). The subsequent psalm verse, taken from Psalm 98:1 (*Notum fecit Dominus . . .*; Psalm 97 in the Latin Vulgate), is then sung by the soloist. In earlier times, the chorus's part of the respond would be repeated, but this practice had disappeared by the 13th century.

Alleluias are performed in a slightly different manner. The soloist intones the opening word (up to the asterisk in the score), then the chorus repeats this same passage exactly. The chorus proceeds to sing the *jubilus*, an elaborate melisma, and the soloist then sings the verse (*Dies sanctificatus . . .*), with the chorus joining in on the final phrase (here, *super terram*). Finally, the soloist sings the opening *alleluia* and the chorus enters directly with the *jubilus*.

3 Plainchant **Vespers on Pentecost Tuesday**

((•─ Listen
CD1   Track 7
mysearchlab
Book p. 38

a) Antiphon *Pacem relinquo vobis*

Peace I leave with you, my peace I give unto you: not as the world giveth, give I unto you. Alleluia.

b) Psalm 116 *Laudate Dominum*

2. Quóniam confirmáta est super nos misericórdia éjus: * et véritas Dómini mánet in *aetér*num.
3. Glória Pátri, et **Fí**lio, * et Spiritu*i* **Sán**cto
4. Sicut érat in princípio, et **nunc**, et **sém**per, * et in saécula saeculó*rum*. Amen.

1. Praise the Lord, all nations; praise Him, all people.
2. For He has bestowed His mercy upon us, and the truth of the Lord endures forever.
3. Glory to the Father and to the Son and to the Holy Spirit
4. As it was in the beginning, is now, and forever, and for generations of generations. Amen.

The chants for the Divine Office (Matins, Lauds, etc.) center on the singing or recitation of Psalms. Traditionally, each recitation in the Divine Office was associated with a more musically varied antiphon. At Vespers on Pentecost (Whitsuntide) Tuesday, for example, Psalm 116 (Vulgate), *Laudate dominum,* was recited to a psalm tone and was both preceded and followed by the antiphon *Pacem reliquo vobis.*

Antiphons tend to be relatively brief. Though syllabic, they are more methodically varied than the psalm recitations they frame. The text for the antiphon *Pacem reliquo vobis* is taken from John 14:27. Composed in Mode 6, *Pacem reliquo vobis* begins and ends on F and covers a melodic span down to the C below and the B♭ above; the necessary flattened fourth step suggests what would later be labeled the "Hypoionian" Mode 10 (which church chant theorists never recognized; see Chapter 4), transposed to F. The melodic intervals are largely conjunct (that is, by step), although there are two leaps of a fifth between C and G (". . . dat, ego . . ."; ". . . vobis, alleluia"). The melody ascends to B♭ before a reinforced descent to C; the closing "alleluia" and Doxology ("Glory be to the Father . . ."), in between the two extremes, settles on the finalis F.

Psalms are recited syllabically to one of the eight melodic formulas known as psalm tones (see textbook Example 1–2). Textually, psalm verses fall into two more or less equal halves, and the music of the psalm tones reflects this structure. (The text of Psalm 116 is unusually brief, with only two verses before the Doxology; most recited psalms are longer.) Each half centers on a recitation tone that is repeated often enough in a mediant (mid-way) cadence, indicated in the notation here with a solid line through the staff: the unshaded square neume can be repeated as needed according to the number of syllables in the text at this point. In the case of the psalm tone used here, there is a related step-wise descent in each half's cadence: the first ends on G, the second on F. This pattern is continued until all the appointed verses of the psalm have been sung.

Performance notes: The two halves of the psalm tone were often sung antiphonally, with the soloist singing the first half of each verse, and the chorus singing the second. At the end of the psalm, the Doxology ("Gloria Patri . . .") would then be sung to the same or similar psalm tone. Originally, the antiphon was repeated after each verse of the psalm; in modern practice, the initial antiphon is followed by only one verse of the psalm, followed by the Doxology. At this point, the original antiphon would be repeated in its entirety. In this way, the antiphon creates what might be thought of as a set of bookends for the psalm.

Notation: The edition here is from one of the modern chant books produced by the monks of Solesmes. Their system of notation retains certain elements of the medieval neumes but can nevertheless be read quite easily with the knowledge of a few simple rules. Each four-line staff is marked with a clef indicating either middle C or the F below middle C. The individual neumes are read from left to right, except for the podatus (♪), which is read from bottom to top. Groupings of notes are sometimes indicated by ligatures (such as ♣ or ♫). What looks like half a neume at the end of each staff line is in fact an indication of the first pitch of the next line. This *custos* ("guardian") makes it easier for the eye to move from one staff to the next.

4 Plainchant Hymn **Pange lingua gloriosi corporis mysterium** (late 13th century)

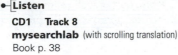

Listen
CD1 Track 8
mysearchlab (with scrolling translation)
Book p. 38

1. Pan - ge lin - gua glo - ri - o - si Cor - po - ris mys - te - ri - um,

San - gui - nis - que pre - ti - o - si, Quem in mun - di pre - ti - um

Fru - ctus ven - tris ge - ne - ro - si Rex ef - fu - dit gen - ti - um.

A - men.

1. Pange lingua gloriosi Corporis mysterium, Sanguinisque pretiosi, Quem in mundi pretium Fructus ventris generosi Rex effudit gentium.	1. Sing, my tongue, the Savior's glory of His flesh the mystery sing; of the Blood, all price exceeding, shed by our immortal King, destined, for the world's redemption, from a noble womb to spring.
2. Nobis datus, nobis natus Ex intacta Virgine, Et in mundo conversatus, Sparso verbi semine, Sui moras incolatus Miro clausit ordine.	2. Of a pure and spotless Virgin born for us on earth below, He, as Man, with man conversing, stayed, the seeds of truth to sow; then He closed in solemn order wondrously His life of woe.
3. In supremae nocte coenae, Recumbens cum fratribus, Observata lege plene Cibis in legalibus, Cibum turbae duodenae Se dat suis manibus.	3. On the night of that Last Supper, seated with His chosen band, He the Paschal victim eating, first fulfills the Law's command; then as Food to His Apostles gives Himself with His own hand.

4. Verbum caro, panem verum
Verbo carnem efficit:
Fitque sanguis Christi merum,
Et si sensus deficit,
Ad firmandum cor sincerum
Sola fides sufficit.

5. Tantum ergo Sacramentum
Veneremur cernui:
Et antiquum documentum
Novo cedat ritui:
Praestet fides supplementum
Sensuum defectui.

6. Genitori, Genitoque
Laus et jubilatio,
Salus, honor, virtus quoque
Sit et benedictio:
Procedenti ab utroque
Compar sit laudatio.
Amen.

(St. Thomas Aquinas, 1225–1274)

4. Word-made-Flesh, the bread of nature
by His word to Flesh He turns;
wine into His Blood He changes;—
what though sense no change discerns?
Only be the heart in earnest,
faith her lesson quickly learns.

5. Down in adoration falling,
Lo! the sacred Host we hail;
Lo! o'er ancient forms departing,
newer rites of grace prevail;
faith for all defects supplying,
where the feeble senses fail.

6. To the everlasting Father,
and the Son who reigns on high,
with the Holy Ghost proceeding
forth from Each eternally,
be salvation, honor, blessing,
might and endless majesty.
Amen.

[from *Liturgia Horarum,*
trans. Fr. Edward Caswall (1814–1878)]

Hymns tend to be syllabic in style. They typically feature multiple strophes, as in the hymn for the Feast of Corpus Christi, *Pange lingua gloriosi corporis mysterium*. Hymns played an important role in the Divine Office. In contrast to liturgical or scriptural texts, hymn texts were newly written and provided an important outlet for the expression of religious ideals and belief. The text of *Pange lingua gloriosi corporis mysterium* was written by none other than Thomas Aquinas (1225–1274), one of the most important theologians of the medieval church. Its melody, by an unknown composer, bears the melodic hallmarks of a later chant style, with a strong sense of melodic symmetry and direction.

((•-|Listen
CD1 Track 9
mysearchlab
Book p. 50

IV

[The Devil attempts to break into the circle of the Virtues to retrieve the Soul, but he is repulsed by them. It would be appropriate for them to repel the Devil by throwing flowers at him.

Victory and Chastity will take up a chain and, with the help of one or more of the other Virtues, will bind the Devil, who will be left lying on the floor until the the end of the production.]

72. The Devil

Que es, aut unde venis?
Who are you, and from whence do you come?

Tu amplexata es me, et ego foras eduxi te.
You have embraced me, and I have led you forth.

Sed nunc in reversione tua confundis me;
But now in your turning back you confuse me;

Ego autem pugna mea deiciam te!
But I will hurl you down with my assault.

73. The Soul, Penitent

E - go om - nes vi - as me - as ma - las es - se co - gno - - vi, et i - de - o fu - gi a
I knew all my ways to be evil, and therefore I ran away

74. The Soul [continuing]

te; mo - do au - tem, o il - lu - sor, pu - gno con - tra te. In - de
from you; now however, O deceiver, I fight against you. Thence,

tu, o re - gi - - - na Hu - mi - li - tas, tu - o me - di - ca -
you, O Queen Humility,

75. Humility to Victory

- mi - ne ad - iu - va me. O Vic - to - ri - a, que i - stum in ce - lo su - -
help me with your medicine. O Victory, who conquered that one [the Devil] in

- pe - ra -sti, cur - - - re cum mi - li - ti - bus tu - - is, et om - nes
heaven, hasten with your knights, and all of you

76. Victory, to the Virtues

li - - ga - te di - a - bo - lum hunc. O for - tis - si - mi et
bind that Devil. O you most brave and

glo - ri - o - sis - si - mi mi - li - tes, ve - ni - te, et ad - iu - va - te me i - stum fal - la -
most glorious knights, come and help me to conquer that deceitful one.

77. Virtues

- cem vin - - ce - re. O dul - cis - si - ma bel - la - - - trix, in tor - ren - te fon - - te
O fairest warrior, who swallowed the greedy wolf in

qui ab -sor - bu - it, lu - pum ra - pa - - - cem! O glo - ri - o - sa co - ro - na -
in the torrent! O glorious crowned one,

- ta, nos li - ben - ter - mi - li - ta - mus te - cum con - tra il - lu - so - rem hunc.
we willingly fight with you against that deceiver.

6   Beatriz de Dia (d. ca. 1212):   **Listen**
A chantar (early 13th century)   CD1   Track 10
mysearchlab (with scrolling translation)
Book p. 53

Hildegard von Bingen's *Ordo virtutum* ("Play of Virtues") is a freely composed drama not connected with any existing chant or ritual but composed instead to texts and melodies entirely of Hildegard's own creation. The plot of this morality play—a dramatized allegory of good versus evil—centers on a series of disputes between the devil and sixteen Virtues, each of which is represented by a different singer. Each character of Hildegard's drama has its own musical profile. "The Penitent Soul," heard at the beginning of this excerpt, sings in a relatively low range when addressing the devil but moves into a higher range when she turns to the Blessed Virgin Mary, the "Queen of Humility." Hildegard also highlights the climactic moment when Satan is bound and thereby symbolically defeated. At this moment, "Victory" sings a high melisma on the word *Gaudete* ("rejoice"). The music up until this point has been largely syllabic and in a lower range. Throughout the entire drama, Satan himself has no music at all: he shouts his lines. It would seem that hell, for Hildegard, was a world without music.

Performance notes: Realizations of Medieval sacred dramas like *Ordo virtutum* are based on sources that transmit only the voice parts, without indication of rhythmic values, much like liturgical chant manuscripts. Some interpretations limit their scope accordingly, using only voices and basing the rhythms on the accents built into the melodic line and text meaning. A few versions add the ringing of bells at the climactic song of Victory ("the old serpent has been bound," section 80). At the other extreme, some performances use an accompanying ensemble (in one case, a flute, a pair of fidels [fiddles], and an organetto), in addition to the bells. Indications of setting and direction are also absent and must be interpolated into any live performance.

A chantar m'es al cor que non deurie
tant mi rancun cele a qui sui amigs,

et si l'am mais que nule ren qui sie;
non mi val ren beltat ni curtesie
ne ma bontaz ne mon pres ne mon sen;
altresi sui enganade et tragide
qu'eusse fait vers lui desavinence.

To sing I must of what I'd rather not,
so much does he of whom I am the lover
    embitter me;
yet I love him more than anything in the world.
To no avail are my beauty or politeness,
my goodness, or my virtue and good sense.
For I have been cheated and betrayed,
as if I had been disagreeable to him.

Forbidden love is a common theme in the poetry of the troubadours and trouvères. It seems to have shaped the life (or at least the writings) of the Countess (Beatriz) de Dia (d. ca. 1212), a *trobairitz* (female troubadour) whose *A chantar m'es al cor* (I must sing from the heart), in Occitan, may well be autobiographical. It is a moving lament written from a woman's perspective, and the only poem of the Countess to have survived in manuscript with music. The music of *A chantar* moves within a relatively narrow ambitus, but its steady rise and fall, culminating in a climb to the melody's highest pitch in the penultimate line, imparts a sense of intense emotion to the words. According to an account (*vida*) written about a century after the Countess's death, she was married to Guillaume, Count of Poitiers, but fell in love with a certain Raimbaut d'Orange (Raimbaut d'Aurenga, d. 1173), also a troubadour, and "made about him many good and beautiful songs"; but chronology and lack of positive evidence make it unlikely that Guillaume or Raimbaut was involved with the Countess.

7 Peire Vidal (fl. 1180–1205): Baros, de mon dan covit (ca. 1200)

((•• Listen

CD1   Track 11
mysearchlab (with scrolling translation)
Book p. 53

Baros, de mon dan covit	My lord, the envious one rejoices
Fa'l lauzengiers deslials,	Over the ills he may now cause.
Qu'en tal domna ai chauzit	For I have chosen a lady
Ont es fis pretz naturals.	Who possesses all natural virtues.
Et ieu am la cor e ses bauzia	I love her completely and openly,
E sui totz sieus, quora qu'ilh sia mia;	And am all hers, if she will be mine;
Quar sa beutat e sa valor pareis,	Her beauty and her worth are so great
Qu'en lieis amar fora honratz us reis,	That a king would be honored to have her:
Per que·m tieng ric sol que·m deinh dire d'oc.	Thus would I hold myself rich were she to accept me.

Anc res tan no m'abellit	Nothing gives me as much joy
Cum sos adreitz cors lials,	As her honorable, faithful loyal heart,
On son tug bon aip complit	So filled with all virtue
E totz bes sense totz mals.	And devoid of all evil.
E pus tot a quan tainh a drudaria,	And since she is so endowed,
Ben sui astrucs, sol que mos cors lai sia;	I shall be happy just to be with her;
E si merces, per que totz bos aips creis,	And if her compassion, highest of all virtues,
Mi val ab lieis, be·us puesc dir ses tozt neis,	Aids my cause, then this virtue
Qu'anc ab amor tant ajudar no·m poc.	Will have played its greatest role in love's success ever.

Regarded highly by his contemporaries and successors, Peire Vidal is credited with around 50 surviving texts; 12 of these have melodies. Many courts sought his talents: he served at the courts of Toulouse, Marseilles, Aragon, Castile, and Montferrat, and he may have accompanied his patron Richard I (Richard the Lion-Hearted) on the Third Crusade (1193–1194). His tempestuous character was far different from that of the Countess, indeed from most troubadours. *Baros, de mon dan covit* ("My lord, he who wishes [my downfall]") begins with typically prodigious praise of a lady, but over the course of the poem Peire compares his behavior at court favorably with others, boasts of his skills in seduction and fighting (which he loves more than monks love peace), and touches on the gossip that surrounds lovers and the imperative to wander. *Baros, de mon dan covit*, like *A chantar*, follows the AAB structure referred to as "bar form" in German medieval secular monophony (discussed earlier in this chapter). Its conjunct melody stays within a fourth for its opening four lines, but then leaps upward dramatically for the fifth and sixth lines ("I love her completely, without falsehood/And am entirely hers, if she will be mine") before returning to the lowest part of the song's ambitus for the final three lines. *A chantar* has seven lines in each stanza and has a tighter melodic structure (a b a b c d b) than *Baros, de mon dan covit*, which after its initial four lines (a a1 a a1) is relatively varied. (See Performance Perspective: Interpreting the Troubadour and Trobairitz Repertory.)

Performance notes: Like other troubadour songs (and those of the trouvères, and sacred dramas like *Ordo virtutum*), only the melody and text are given here (and numerous texts without music, and music without texts, survive). Performances for solo voice are rarely heard today in medieval secular repertory; the issue becomes choice of accompaniment, whether single instruments or an ensemble, and what family or families (string, wind, percussion) will achieve musical goals.

8 Alfonso el Sabio (?) (1221–84):
Cantigas de Santa Maria,
no. 140: A Santa Maria dadas
(ca. 1270–1290)

((•• Listen
CD1   Track 12
mysearchlab (with scrolling translation)
Book p. 54

A Santa Maria dadas
sejan loores onrradas.

1. Loemos a sa mesura,
   seu prez e sa apostura,
   e seu sen e sa cordura,
   mui máis ca cen mil vegadas.
   A Santa Maria...

2. Loemos a sa nobreza,
   sa onrra e sa alteza,
   sa mercee e sa franqueza,
   e sas vertudes preçadas.
   A Santa Maria...

3. Loemos sa lealdade,
   seu conort' e sa bondade,
   seu acorr' e sa verdade,
   con loores mui cantadas.
   A Santa Maria...

To Holy Mary be
given respectful praises.

Let us praise her dignity,
her worth and her gracefulness,
5 and her judgment and her wisdom,
much more than a hundred thousand times.
   To Holy Mary...

Let us praise her nobility,
her honour and her rank,
10 her mercy and her openness,
and her treasured virtues.
   To Holy Mary...

Let us praise her loyalty,
her consolation and her bounty,
15 her help and her truth,
with praises ever sung.
   To Holy Mary...

4. Loemos seu cousimento,
consell' e castigamento,
seu ben, seu ensinamento
e sas graças mui grãadas.
A Santa Maria...

Let us praise her attentiveness,
her counsel and admonition,
20 her goodness, her learning
and her graces so fine.
To Holy Mary...

5. Loando-a, que nos valla
lle roguemos na batalla
do mundo que nos traballa,
e do dem' a denodadas.
A Santa Maria...

In praising her, let us ask her
that she be a strength to us in the battle
25 against this world, which causes us travail,
and against the devil, with valour.
To Holy Mary...

The preserved repertory of *cantigas* ("songs") from the Iberian Peninsula—present-day Spain and Portugal—is quite small. Only two sources transmit the poetry with melodies. One of these is a large and sumptuously illustrated manuscript containing more than 400 *Cantigas de Santa Maria,* songs in Honor of the Virgin Mary (see illustration, textbook, p. 56). This source was prepared for (and possibly composed in part by) Alfonso el Sabio ("The Wise"), king of Castille and Leon from 1252 until 1284. Although sacred in subject matter, these songs were not liturgical. Their poetic and musical style, moreover, is consistent with what we know of the secular songs that were written in this place and time. The texts of the *cantigas* are written in Gallo-Portuguese, and most are set syllabically in strophic form with a refrain.

Scholars have debated the extent of Arabic influence on the music of this repertory. Large portions of the Iberian Peninsula had been under Muslim rule since the 8th century, and the impact of this culture on the regions of what are now Spain and Portugal extended to virtually every aspect of life. Exactly how much musical influence is to be found in the *Cantigas de Santa Maria* remains unclear, however.

Performance notes: The accompanying instrument heard on this recording is a dulcimer, a zither-like instrument. The fact that only the vocal line is preserved in notated form in no way precludes the addition of one or more instruments that might serve to introduce the voice and double its line.

9 | Walther von der Vogelweide
(ca. 1170–1230):
Palästinalied (ca. 1200)

((•─Listen
CD1 Track 13
mysearchlab (with scrolling translation)
Book p. 56

1. Nu alest leb' ich mir werde,
sît mîn sundic ouge ersiht.
Lant daz hêre und ouch die erde,
dem man vil der êren giht.

Mir'st geschehn, des ich ie bat,
ich bin komen an die stat,
da got mennischlîchen trat.

1. Now for the first time I am alive,
For my sinful eyes have beheld
the land here and the very earth
to which mankind gives such honor.

I have that for which I so long prayed,
I have come to the place
where God walked as man.

In German-speaking lands, the *Minnesinger* (literally, singers of *Minne,* or "courtly love") developed their own repertory of songs. Walther von der Vogelweides *Palästinalied* provides a good example of this repertory. Chivalry, the praise of God, and the praise of noblewomen are recurrent themes in this repertory. Like many *Minnelieder* (*Lieder* means "songs"), Walther's *Palästinalied* is written in bar form, consisting of two musically identical statements (called *Stollen*) and a final closing statement (the *Abgesang*), creating the pattern of AAB. It is largely syllabic, and it tells of a crusader knight's thrill at standing on the same ground as Christ had during his lifetime. (The First Crusade had captured Jerusalem in 1099, permitting Christians to make pilgrimages to the holy city.) Like the songs of the troubadours and trouvères, the *Minnelieder* were almost certainly performed to the accompaniment of instruments, but no notated source of this accompaniment has been preserved.

Performance notes: The plucked instrument heard in the accompaniment is an 'ud, a short-necked lute without frets common in northern Africa and the Middle East. It is a forerunner of the lute, whose name is a corruption of the French *l'ud* ("the 'ud"). The bowed stringed instrument is a rebec, a small, three-stringed instrument also of Middle Eastern origin.

10 Melismatic organum **Kyrie Cunctipotens genitor deus**
(ca. 1120–1130)

((•─ **Listen**

CD1   Track 14
mysearchlab (with scrolling translation)
Book p. 60

Cunctipotens genitor Deus, omni creator, eleison.
Fons et origo boni pie luxque perennis, eleison.
Salvificet pietas tua nos bone rector, eleison.
Christe Dei forma virtus Patrisque sophia, eleison.
Plasmatis humani factor lapsi reparator, eleison.
Ne tua damnetur jhesu factura benigne, eleison.
Amborum sacrum spiramen nexus amorque, eleison.
Procedens fomes vitae fons purificans vis, eleison.
Purgator culpe venie largitor opimae, offensas dele sancto nos munere reple spiritus alme.

Omnipotent Father, God, creator of all, have mercy.
Fountain and origin of all good, holy and eternal light, have mercy.
May your holiness bring us salvation, O good Leader, have mercy.
Christ, appearance of God, power and wisdom of the Father, have mercy.
Maker of human flesh, savior of the fallen, have mercy.
Let not your creation be damned, O goodly Jesus.
Sacred breath of both, and combined love, have mercy.
Active former of life, fountain purifying us, have mercy.
Redeemer of sin, greatest dispenser of pardon, remove our misdeeds, fill us with holy reward, O nurturing Spirit.

New edition by Samuel Brannon from the Codex Calixtinus, f. 190r. Additional text from *Analecta hymnica medii aevi*, ed. Clemens Blume and Guido M. Drewes, vol. 47, *Tropi gradualis* (Leipzig: O. R. Reisland, 1905), p. 50.

Melismatic organum introduced multiple notes in the *vox organalis* against a single note in the original plainchant. This type of organum is particularly prevalent in manuscripts from northern Spain and from southwestern France, particularly the abbey of St. Martial, in what is now southern France. The two-part organum *Kyrie Cunctipotens genitor deus* comes from the Codex Calixtinus, a text written around 1120–1130 as a guide and songbook for pilgrims on their way to Santiago de Compostela, the site of the shrine of Saint James the Apostle, in what is now northwestern Spain. The lower voice of this organum built on the plainchant Kyrie *Cunctipotens genitor deus* (Anthology I/2b). The upper voice is freely composed, while the text glosses the basic idea of the Kyrie, a prayer for mercy.

Performance notes: While the pitches of the original notation are fairly clear, the alignment of the two voices is often ambiguous. The edition here suggests one possible approach. The opening and closing harmonies of each melodic unit (demarcated by a rest in the score) are always consonant at the unison, fifth, or octave; the way in which the two voices converge in the middle of each phrase remains open to interpretation.

11 Léonin (?) (fl. mid- to late 12th century): Two-Voice Organum **Viderunt omnes**
(mid- to late 12th century)

((•• Listen
CD1 Track 15
mysearchlab (with scrolling translation)
Book p. 61

O.L. 267

O.L. 267

R. Haec dies [quam fecit dominus: exsultemus
   et laetemur in ea.]

V. Confitemini Domino, quoniam bonus: quoniam
   in saeculum [misericordia eius].

R. This is the day [which the Lord hath made;
   let us rejoice and be glad in it.]

V. Give thanks unto the Lord; for he is good:
   for [his mercy] endureth forever.

(Ps. 118: 24, 29) N.B. The text in brackets is
performed in plainchant, not organum, and
therefore does not appear in the original score.

The most elaborate forms of Medieval organum appeared from a circle of largely anonymous composers working in and around the Cathedral of Notre Dame in Paris in the 12th century. Léonin (or Leoninus, in the Latinized form) and Pérotin (Perotinus) are the only two composers of this repertory whose names we know.

O.L. 267

Léonin and his colleagues turned their attention primarily to the responsorial chants—that is, those plainchants performed in part by a soloist (or small group of soloists singing in unison), to which a chorus responds. Léonin left unchanged the choral portions of these chants, which continued to be performed monophonically by the chorus, but he wrote lengthy two-voice organa for those portions of the chants performed by the soloists. His organum setting of the Christmas Day plainchant Gradual *Viderunt omnes* (Anthology I/2d) may be diagrammed as follows:

RESPOND		VERSE	
soloists	Chorus	soloists	Chorus
Two-part organum	Plainchant	Two-part organum	Plainchant
Viderunt omnes	*fines terrae . . .*	*Notum fecit . . .*	*iustitiam.*

Léonin's organal sections are either in melismatic organum (also known as free organum or unmeasured organum) or in measured organum (also known as discant organum). In free organum, the duplum voice moves rapidly against the slower moving notes of the original chant. It was used in passages that in the original chant are neumatic, as on the opening word *Viderunt*. In measured organum, the two voices move at about the same speed in what is essentially a note-against-note style. This type of organum was used in passages that are melismatic in the original chant, such as on the word *omnes* (in *Viderunt omnes*) and, in the verse, on the word *Dominus*.

Performance notes: As is so often the case in early polyphony, questions of rhythmic interpretation are far more troublesome than questions of pitch. The edition here interprets the entire organum in modern-day notation; but this does not reflect the kind of rhythmic fluidity that was probably used in actual performances of organum during the 12th century, particularly in the sections of free organum (as at the beginning, m. 1–51). The measured organum (m. 70–98, for example) is somewhat better served by this form of notation; the rhythmic coordination of the two voices here is less ambiguous. Some recent performances of organum have doubled the sustained lower voices with instruments, but there is some controversy over whether or not this would have been the practice in the medieval church. The recording here is entirely vocal.

12 Pérotin (fl. late 12th century): Four-voice Organum **Viderunt omnes** (late 12th century)

((•• Listen

CD1   Track 16

mysearchlab (with scrolling translation)

Book p. 62

O.L. 261

O.L. 261

4

O.L. 261

O.L. 261

- nes   fi - nes ter - - re

sa - lu - ta - - re   de - - i   no - stri

iu - bi - la - te   de - - o   om -

- nis   ter - - ra.

O.L. 261

O.L. 261

No. 12   Pérotin: Four-voice Organum Viderunt omnes   ■

O.L. 261

O.L. 261

O.L. 261

O.L. 261

O.L. 261

O.L. 261

Once the basic principles of polyphonic composition and notation had been established, composers were able to add still further layers of musical commentary to their original glosses on a given chant. The composer known only as Pérotin (Perotinus), a younger contemporary of Léonin, is credited with having added a third voice (known as the triplum) and on rare occasions even a fourth voice (quadruplum) to organa for feasts of special significance. These are works of astonishing length. Even in a fairly lively performance, such as the one here, Pérotin's four-voice organum for the Gradual *Viderunt omnes* runs more than 11 minutes, with the first word of the text—*Viderunt*—drawn out for more than two full minutes. The original melody of the plainchant, in the tenor voice, is sung to extremely long notes that serve as a foundation to the superstructure of the three upper voices, which intertwine in a higher and relatively narrow range and at a far more rapid pace. Each syllable of the first word brings out a new vowel sound—*Vi* ("ee")-*de* ("eh")-*runt* (short "u")—which in turn changes the sonority of the whole. The tenor voice also shifts pitch with each new syllable, furthering a sense of forward motion. In this way, a single word of three syllables intoned over a span of more than two minutes conveys a sense of enormous variety and momentum.

The return to plainchant at the words *finis terr[a]e* corresponds to the point of the original plainchant Gradual at which the chorus begins its response to the opening words of the soloist (*Viderunt omnes*). The organal portions of Pérotin's setting were probably sung by soloists or a small ensemble of singers with only a few voices to each part: this is rhythmically intricate music that demands a higher level of musical skill than that possessed by the average monk. Polyphony returns with the verse *Notum fecit . . . .* At the word *Dominus*, the tenor voice assumes a strict rhythmic pattern for this first time; this corresponds to the similar change from free to strict rhythm at the same point in the earlier two-voice organum. This change, too, helps propel the music forward and give it a sense of ever-building energy, even as it seems to otherwise operate somehow outside the parameters of time. If we can imagine ourselves back in the 12th century, hearing polyphony for the first time, and in a setting as grand and vast as the Cathedral of Notre Dame in Paris, we can begin to appreciate the power of this music to enhance the spiritual qualities of the liturgy. And we can understand why such extraordinary works like Pérotin's four-voice organum on *Viderunt omnes* were reserved for special feasts of the liturgical year, such as Christmas Day.

No. 12 Pérotin: Four-voice Organum Viderunt omnes ■ 23

13 Two-voice Clausula on "Dominus" (late 12th century?)

((•─Listen
CD1   Track 17
mysearchlab
Book p. 63

The drive to gloss did not end with the composition of organum, not even for three and four voices. Composers like Pérotin also composed many clausulae—brief polyphonic sections of discant organum—that could be substituted at will into the appropriate section of a larger existing work of organum. The clausula (to use its singular form) is thus not an independent composition that can be performed on its own. The tenor voice of a typical clausula in fact often consists of only a single word or even just a syllable or two of a longer word. The clausula here, for example, consists of a single word, *Dominus* (Lord).

A single source typically provides clausulae for several different passages within the same organum and sometimes even multiple clausulae for the same passage. The Florence manuscript of the *Magnus liber organi*, for example, contains no fewer than nine different two-voice clausulae for the passage on the words *Dominus* within the Gradual *Viderunt omnes*. Clausulae could be longer, shorter, or about the same length as the passage they were written to replace. Stylistically, however, clausulae are always in the same style of organum as the passage into which they could be inserted. In the complete two-voice organum of the Gradual *Viderunt omnes*, for example, the word *Dominus* is set in measured organum, and the many clausulae that might be substituted for this passage are also in measured organum.

In performing organum, singers were free to substitute whichever clausula or clausulae they desired in any combination. Alternatively, they could use no clausulae at all and sing the organum in its original form. What is important here from a liturgical point of view is that regardless of the clausulae chosen (or not chosen), all the notes and words of the original chant would be present in one form or another. The impetus for clausulae, as for organa, it would seem, lay in the desire to write new music that would gloss the original plainchant by providing different layers of musical "commentary" above the plainchant.

14 Motet **Factum est salutare / Dominus** (13th century)

((•● Listen
CD1   Track 18
mysearchlab (with scrolling translation)
Book p. 66

Factum est salutare / Dominus

Factum est salutare	Salvation was made known
conspectu notum gentium.	in the sight of the peoples.
A rege mundus Cesare	The world called Caesar the
describit auctor omnium.	author of all things.
Rex nascit salvare	The king [i.e., Christ] was born to save
quidam ut ergo Lazare	those who therefore like Lazarus
post triduum iam compare.	appear again after three days.
Tardare nimis fatuum	To excessively delay healing the foolish [i.e., the heathen]
sanare quartum mortuum	who are dead four days
numquam voluit Dominus.	was never wished by the Lord.

Although clausulae may have been fragmentary from a liturgical point of view, consisting of only a few syllables or words, the longer ones constituted a musical whole that began and ended in the same mode; the very word clausula itself comes from a Latin root meaning "to cadence" or "conclude." The only thing many clausulae lacked to be performed separately was a text.

In the venerable medieval tradition of troping, some unknown individual or group of individuals working in the late 12th or early 13th century had the idea of underlaying a new text to the duplum of an existing clausula and performing the new work outside the liturgy of the church. Thus was born the genre of the motet (from the French word *mot*, meaning "word"). The term was fitting because the text for the duplum in many of the earliest motets was in the vernacular, not Latin. It is the presence of a contrasting text in the upper voice or voices that distinguishes the motet from its immediate ancestor, the clausula. The texted duplum was known as the motetus because it had words. Musically, there are only minor differences between the clausula on *Dominus* (Anthology I/13) and the motet *Factum est salutare/Dominus*. (By convention, the titles of 13th-century motets consist of the first word or words of each voice in order from top to bottom.) The Latin text for the motetus is a trope on the longer text in which the word *Dominus* originally appeared, the plainchant Gradual for the Mass on Christmas Day. The musical differences between the original clausula and the motet are so minor, in fact, that one can easily follow a performance of the latter using the score of the former. Once again, we see the urge of medieval minds to gloss an existing text (or in this case, an exsting text and melody) by adding new layers.

((•—Listen
CD1 Track 19
mysearchlab (with scrolling translation)
Book p. 66

O.L.235

Triplum
Super te Jerusalem
de matre virgine
ortus est in Bethle[h]em
deus in homine;
ut gyga substancie
processit gemine
virginis ex utero
sine gravamine.
Non fuit feconditas
hec viri semine.

Duplum
Sed fulsit virginitas
de sancto flamine.
Ergo, pie virginis
flos, pie domine,
da medelam criminis
matris pro nomine
ne nos preda demonis
simus pro crimine
quos preciosi sanguinis
emisti flumine.

Primus Tenor
[untexted]

Secundus Tenor
Dominus.

Over you, Jerusalem
God has arisen,
becoming a man of a virgin mother
in Bethlehem;
he came forth
like a giant of twin substance
from the virgin's womb
without pain.
This fertility was not caused
by the seed of a man.

But her virginity
took flame from the holy fire.
Therefore, O merciful Lord,
flower of a merciful virgin,
give us the remedy for our sin
for the sake of your mother's name
lest we, whom you have bought
with the river
of your precious blood,
become the devil's prey through sin.

Lord.

Separated from its liturgical context, the tenor of a motet was no longer a sacred object—a portion of a larger plainchant—and composers were quick to take advantage of this fact. They began to manipulate the musical content of the tenor in various ways. The movement in this direction is evident in the four-part motet *Super te / Sed fulsit / Primus tenor / Dominus*: its lowest voice is based on the familiar *Dominus tenor* (see Anthology I/13 and I/14) but with the rhythms and even some of the pitches treated rather freely at points. Someone—an anonymous composer, possibly working in England around 1270—also added a second, untexted tenor to create a four-voice texture. The upper two voices (in Latin) sing two different texts, each of which is a gloss on the Christmas story, with emphasis on the miracle of the virgin birth of Christ. The end result is a self-contained whole, a set of multiple glosses on a single theme, both from the literary and musical point of view. This polytextual motet is typical of the genre in the second half of the 13th century: different voices sing different texts simultaneously.

16 Motet A Paris / On parole / Frese nouvele (late 13th century)

((•◦ Listen

CD1   Track 20
mysearchlab (with scrolling translation)
Book p. 67

Triplum

1. On parole de batre et de vanner
2. et de foïr et de hanner;
3. mais ces deduis trop me desplaisent,
4. car il n'est si bone vie que d'estre a aise
5. de bon cler vin et de chapons
6. et d'estre aveuc bons compaignons,
7. liés et joiaus,
8. chantans, truffans et amorous,
9. et d'avoir, quant a mestier,
10. pour solacier
11. beles dames a devis:
12. Et tout ce truev[e] on a Paris.

Triplum

1. One speaks of threshing and winnowing,
2. of toiling and puffing,
3. but these displease me much,
4. for there is nothing as good as being filled
5. with good clear wine and capons,
6. and to be with good friends,
7. merry and jolly,
8. singing, stuffed, amorous,
9. and having all one might need
10. to delight
11. beautiful women as one wishes:
12. And all this one finds in Paris

Duplum

1. A Paris soir et matin
2. truev[e] on bon pain et bon cler vin,
3. bone char et bon poisson,
4. de toutes guises compaignons,
5. sens soutie, grant baudour,
6. biaus joiaus dames d'ounour;
7. et si truev[e] on bien entredeus
8. de menre feur pour homes desiteus.

Duplum

1. In Paris, night and morning,
2. One finds good bread and good, clear wine,
3. good meat and good fish,
4. all kinds of friends,
5. with lively minds and great spirits,
6. noble ladies quite merry;
7. and one finds all this with
8. prices to suit a man without means.

Tenor

1. Frese nouvele, muere france, muere, muere france!
2. Frese nouvele, muere france, muere, muere france!
3. Frese nouvele, muere france, muere, muere france!
4. Frese nouvele, muere france, muere, muere france!

Tenor

1. Fresh strawberries, nice blackberries!
2. Fresh strawberries, nice blackberries!
3. Fresh strawberries, nice blackberries!
4. Fresh strawberries, nice blackberries!

The anonymous motet *A Paris / On parole / Frese nouvele* bears no relationship at all to any pre-existing work. It is based on a newly composed tenor with its own self-contained (if very brief) text in French. The tenor states its eight-measure unit of text and music a total of four times. At least one of the two upper voices, in turn, overlaps the cadential points of the tenor, thus creating a sense of forward momentum even while articulating points of rest within the three-voice texture. The text of the tenor—*Frese nouvele, muere france* ("Fresh strawberries! Nice blackberries!")—is a street vendor's call, the 13th-century equivalent of a peanut vendor's cry in a baseball stadium. As such, it justifies both the musical and textual repetition it receives here.

The motetus and triplum of this same motet present two texts different from each other and different yet again from that of the tenor. The resulting polytextual motet is typical of the genre in the second half of the 13th century. The three texts of *A Paris / On parole / Frese nouvele* are all related in content. Above the street-vendor's cry in the tenor, the triplum and duplum extol the virtues of Paris: good bread, good wine, good friends, even good prices "to suit a poor man's purse." The texts of many other 13th-century motets are more diverse; some are even polyglot, with a motetus in Latin and a triplum in French, or vice versa. Subject matter is often equally unrelated. It is not unusual, for example, to find a sacred Latin motetus juxtaposed with a French triplum whose text is a love poem. The distinction between sacred and secular was not nearly so sharp in the medieval era as it would be in later centuries. Still, one senses in at least some of these compositions a real delight in the contrasting images they evoke. It is also likely that they contain references that would have been familiar in the 13th century but are no longer readily grasped today.

Performance notes: The ensemble here consists of three solo (male) voices, using pronunciation believed to be more consistent with the way French would have been spoken in the 13th century. At the very end, for example, we hear "Paris" with an audible "s," rather than in the modern French pronunciation ("Pa-ree").

17 Conductus **Flos ut rosa floruit** ((••⌐Listen
(second half of 13th century)

CD1   Track 21
mysearchlab (with scrolling translation)
Book p. 68

I. Flos ut rosa floruit, quando Virgo genuit
   Maria
   Salvatorem omnium, summi Patris Filium,
   nova genitura.

I. A flower bloomed like a rose, when the
   Virgin Mary gave birth
   To the Savior of all people, the Son of the
   highest Father, *in a birth of utter newness.*

II. Qui divina gracia descendit ad infera
    humana,
    Et salvavit omnia summa cum potencia,
    nova genitura.

II. In divine grace he came down to humanity
    below
    And saved us all with his immense power, *in
    a birth of utter newness.*

III. Cantemus hymnum glorie, cantico
     leticie laudando,
     Sollempnizantes hodie regi regum iusticie
     gracias agendo.

III. Let us sing a hymn of glory, praising him
     with a song of joy,
     And celebrate today by giving thanks to the
     justice of the king of kings.

IV. Qui natus est de virgine mistico spiramine,
    nova genitura.
    Ergo nostra concio psallat cum tripudio
    benedicat Domino.

IV. He was born of a virgin by a mystical spirit,
    in a birth of utter newness.
    Therefore let this group dance and sing
    praises and bless the Lord.

The conductus offered yet another outlet for composers wishing to write either monophonic or polyphonic music in the late 12th and early 13th centuries. These works, for one, two, three, or occasionally four voices, are not based on borrowed material of any kind. The texts consist of freely composed poetry written in metered verse that lend themselves to syllabic and strongly metrical musical settings. In the polyphonic conductus, all voices move in roughly the same rhythm. The note-against-note part-writing in this genre is so distinctive in fact that this manner of composition in medieval music has since come to be called "conductus style." Conducti (or conductus; both can be used as plurals) derive their name from the Latin word *conducere,* meaning "to escort," and these pieces were probably first used as processionals—that is, as music to be performed while a priest and his attendants entered and left the church.

Rhythmically, the notation of these pieces is ambiguous. They do not follow the system of modal rhythm evident in the measured sections of organum, clausula, and motet, but probably adhere to the modal rhythm of the texts themselves. Most sources align the voices with some care, using vertical lines to clarify the relationship of the different parts. The long melisma at the end of the last strophe of *Flos ut rosa floruit* is a characteristic feature of the genre known as a *cauda,* a term derived from the Latin word for "tail," the same root word from which "coda" would eventually evolve.

18   Philippe de Vitry (?) (1291–1361):
      Motet **Garrit Gallus / In nova
      fert / Neuma** (ca. 1315)

((•–Listen
CD1   Track 22
mysearchlab (with scrolling translation)
Book p. 77

No. 18 Philippe de Vitry: Motet Garrit Gallus / In nova fert / Neuma ■ 31

TRIPLUM

Garrit Gallus flendo dolorose
Luget quippe Gallorum concio.
Que satrape traditur dolose,
Ex cubino sedens officio.
Atque vulpes, tamquam vispilio
in Belial vigens astucia
De leonis consensu proprio
Monarchisat, atat angaria
Rursus, ecce. Jacob familia
Pharaone altero fugatur;
Non ut olim lude vestigia
Subintrare potens, lacrimatur.
In deserto fame flagellatur.
Adiutoris carens armatura.
Quamquam clamat, tamen spoliatur,
Continuo forsan moritura.

The cock babbles, lamenting sorrowfully,
for the whole assembly of cocks*
mourns because, while serving vigilantly,
it is trickily betrayed by the satrap.
And the fox,† like a grave robber,
thriving with the astuteness of Belial,
rules as a monarch with the consent
of the lion himself.‡ Ah, what slavery!
Lo, once again Jacob's family
is exiled by another Pharaoh.
Not, as formerly, able to escape
to the homeland of Judah, they weep.
Stricken by hunger in the desert,
lacking the help of arms,
although they cry out, they are robbed;
perhaps speedily they will die.

* Gallus: cock; or Gauls (the French)
† Enguerran de Marigny, chief councillor of the
French king
‡ Philip IV the Fair

O miserum exulum vox dura!
O Gallorum garritus doloris,
Cum leonis cecitas obscura
Fraudi paret vulpis proditioris.
Eius fastus sustinens erroris
Insurgito: alias labitur
Et labetur quod haves honoris,
Quod mox in facinis tardis ultoribus itur.

O harsh voice of the wretched exiles;
O sorrowful babbling of the cocks,
since the dark blindness of the lion
submits to the fraud of the traitorous fox.
You who suffer the arrogance of his misdeeds,
rise up,
or what you have of honor is being or
will be lost, because if avengers are slow
men soon turn to evil doing.

DUPLUM

In nova fert animus mutatas
Dicere formas.
Draco nequam quam olim penitus
Mirabilis crucis potencia
Debellavit Michael inclitus,
Mox Absalon munitus gracia,
Mox Ulixis gaudens facundia,
Mox lupinis dentibus armatus,
Sub Tersitis miles milicia
Rursus vivit in vulpem mutatus,
Cauda cuius, lumine privatus
Leo, vulpe imperante, paret.
Oves suggit pullis saciatus.

Heu! suggere non cessat et aret
Ad nupcias carnibus non caret.
Ve pullis mox, ve ceco leoni!
Coram Christotandem ve draconi.

My heart is set upon speaking of forms
changed into new (bodies).§
The evil dragon that renowned Michael once
utterly defeated by the miraculous power
of the Cross,
now endowed with the grace of Absalom,
now with the cheerful eloquence of Ulysses,
now armed with wolfish teeth
a soldier in the service of Thersites,
lives again changed into a fox
whose tail the lion deprived
of sight obeys, while the fox reigns.
He sucks the blood of sheep and is satiated
with chickens.
Alas, he does not cease sucking and still thirsts;
he does not abstain from meats at the wedding feast.
Woe now to the chickens, woe to the blind lion.
In the presence of Christ, finally, woe to the dragon.

—RICHARD HOPPIN

§ Ovid *Metamorphoses*,1,1.

One of the twelve surviving manuscripts of the *Roman de Fauvel* includes a number of interpolated musical compositions, ranging from short, monophonic pieces to large-scale polyphonic motets. The polyglot (multilingual) motet *Garrit gallus / In nova fert / Neuma* may be by Philippe de Vitry himself, who refers to it in his treatise *Ars nova* to illustrate certain features of the *ars nova* or "new art."

The untexted tenor of *Garrit gallus / In nova fert / Neuma* is freely composed and bears the simple indication *Neuma,* a kind of generic designation for a melisma. The tenor is structured according to the principle of isorhythm, a term coined in the 20th century to describe a technique common to many motets and mass movements written between roughly 1300 and 1450. An isorhythmic tenor is one based on a fixed rhythmic and melodic pattern that is repeated at least once (and usually more often) over the course of an entire work. Isorhythm became the preferred structure of the motet in the 14th century.

The rhythmic pattern of an isorhythmic tenor is called its *talea* (meaning "cutting" or "segment"); the melodic pattern is called its *color* (a term borrowed from rhetoric and used to describe certain techniques of repetition). Although *talea* and *color* are sometimes of the same length within a given tenor, more often they are not. The *talea* of the tenor of *Garrit gallus / In nova fert / Neuma* (see the example) is stated six times in succession, beginning at measures 1, 11, 21, 31, 41, and 51. The *color,* in contrast, is three times as long and is stated in its entirety only twice, beginning at measures 1 and 31.

The *talea* of the tenor in *Garrit gallus / In nova fert / Neuma*.

**19 Guillaume de Machaut
(ca. 1300–1377): Messe de
Nostre Dame: Kyrie (ca. 1360)**

((•—Listen
CD1   Track 23
mysearchlab
Book p. 78

three times

Guillaume de Machaut's *Messe de Nostre Dame* ("Mass of Our Lady") is the only 14th-century polyphonic setting of the complete Mass Ordinary known to have been written by a specific composer. Machaut differentiates between movements with large quantities of text and those with relatively little text. The former are set in a predominantly syllabic, conductuslike fashion (note-against-note), while the latter are set in the style of an isorhythmic motet. Whatever their differences in style, all the movements are based on a plainchant version of the appropriate element of the Ordinary. Thus the tenor of the isorhythmic Kyrie derives from the plainchant Kyrie *Cunctipotens Genitor Deus* (see Anthology I/10). The *talea* (the rhythmic pattern) of the tenor in the first Kyrie is extremely brief (only four measures in modern transcription), and the only rest comes at the very end of the *talea,* which helps articulate each successive return. The *color* (the melodic pattern), adhering to the pitches of the chant exactly, is stated only once. In a practice that became common around the middle of the 14th century, Machaut includes a voice known as the contratenor (meaning "against the tenor") that occupies the same range as the tenor. The contratenor, like the tenor, is isorhythmic, but its *talea* in the first Kyrie is longer. It is fully stated twice—in m. 1–12 and 13–25—then restated partially in the last two measures. By virtue of its length and internal rests, it keeps the motion of the lower voices moving forward. The *color* of the contratenor, unrelated to any preexisting melody, is stated only once. The motetus (duplum) and triplum move freely in more rapid rhythms. In the Christe and the final Kyrie, the *talea* of the tenor and contratenor voices coincide.

The melodic character of Machaut's Kyrie is typical of mid-14th-century polyphony: somewhat angular, with large leaps (an upward seventh in the contratenor of Kyrie I in m. 17, an upward major sixth in m. 21–22), hockets (from the Latin word for "hiccough") in m. 10 and 22, and a good deal of syncopation throughout.

The principal cadences follow the standard formulas of the day, with the two structural voices—the highest-sounding voice and the tenor, which together provide the basic harmonic intervals—moving from a sixth to an octave or from a third to a fifth. Such cadences are found in Machaut's Kyrie at m. 80 (sixth to an octave in the tenor and the triplum, the highest-sounding voice at this point) and at m. 27 (third to fifth in the tenor and triplum).

0:46

1. Je puis trop bien ma dame comparer
2. A l'image que fist Pymalion.
3. D'ivoire fu, tant belle et si sans per
4. Que plus l'ama que Medée Jazon.
5. Li folz toudis la prioit,
6. Mais l'image riens ne le respondoit.
7. Einse me fait celle qui mon cuer font,

8. *Qu'ades la pri et riens ne me respont.*

I can all too well compare my lady
To the image which Pygmalion made.
It was of ivory, so beautiful, without peer,
That he loved it more than Jason did Medea.
Out of his senses, he prayed to it unceasingly,
But the image answered him not.
Thus does she, who makes my heart melt, treat me,
For I implore her ever, and she answers me not.

By the middle of the 14th century, three *formes fixes*—literally "fixed forms," or structural patterns—had established themselves as the most important varieties of secular song in France: the ballade, virelai, and the rondeau. These were at once both poetic and musical forms, each with its own characteristic pattern of rhyme and musical repetition, with at least one line of refrain—that is, the same words sung to the same music in every strophe (or verse). Musically, each of these forms consists of two parts, conventionally labeled A and B. The first ending of a repeated part (A, B, or both) is known as its *ouvert* ("open") and the second ending as its *clos* ("close").

The text of the ballade usually consists of three strophes of seven or eight lines, the last of which is a refrain. The rhyme pattern varies. That of Machaut's ballade *Je puis trop bien ma dame comparer* ("I may well compare my lady") is ababccdD. (Lowercase letters indicate lines of text that are different in each strophe; uppercase letters indicate the refrain, which is identical throughout, both textually and musically.) Other typical rhyme patterns for the ballade include ababbcbC, ababcdE, and ababcdeF.

Musically, the ballade falls into two distinct sections, the first of which is always repeated and the second of which is sometimes repeated. The music thus unfolds in the pattern AAB (like Machaut's *Je puis trop bien ma dame comparer,* see the following table) or AABB.

STROPHE 1	RHYME SCHEME	MUSICAL STRUCTURE
RELATION OF TEXT AND MUSICAL STRUCTURE IN MACHAUT'S BALLADE *JE PUIS TROP BIEN MA DAME COMPARER*		
Je puis trop bien ma dame comparer	a	A, first ending (*ouvert*)
A l'ymage que fist Pymalion.	b	
D'yvoire fu, tant belle et si sans per	a	A, second ending (*clos*)
Que plus l'ama que Medea Jazon.	b	
Li folz toudis la prioit,	c	B
Mais l'ymage riens ne lie respondoit.	c	
Einsi me fait celle qui mon cuer font,	d	
Qu'ades la pri et riens ne me respont.	D (refrain)	

Ballades tend to be the most melismatic of all the *formes fixes* used in 14th-century France, with a rhythmically active uppermost voice. Machaut's *Je puis trop* is highly florid, yet the cadences are carefully aligned to the structure of the poetry. As in Machaut's four-part setting of the Mass, the tenor and contratenor lines weave in and out of one another.

21 Guillaume de Machaut: Virelai
Douce dame jolie
(ca. 1330–1350?)

((• Listen
CD1   Track 25
mysearchlab (with scrolling translation)
Book p. 81

Douce dame jolie,		Fair sweet lady,
Pour Dieu ne pensés mie		for God's sake do not think
Que nulle ait signourie		that any woman has mastery
Seur moy, fors vous seulement.		over me, save you alone.

i	Qu'adès sans tricherie Chierie	For always without deceit I have cherished you,
	Vous ay, et humblement Tous les jours de ma vie Servie	and humbly served you all the days of my life
	Sans vilein pensement.	without any base thought.
	Helas! et je mendie D'esperance et d'aïe; Dont ma joie est fenie, Se pité ne vous en prent.	Alas! I am bereft of hope and help; and so my joy is ended, unless you pity me.

Dous dame jolie . . .

ii	Mais vo douce maistrie Maistrie Mon cuer si durement Qu'elle le contralie Et lie En amours, tellement	But your sweet mastery masters my heart so harshly as to torment it and bind it with love, so much so
	Qu'il n'a de riens envie Fors d'estre en vo baillie; Et se ne li ottrie Vos cuers nul aligement.	that it desires nothing but to be in your power; and yet your heart grants it no relief.

Douce dame jolie . . .

iii	Et quant ma maladie Garie Ne sera nullement Sans vous, douce anemie, Qui lie Estes de mon tourment.	And since my sickness will not be cured in any way save by you, sweet enemy, who are glad at my distress,
	A jointes mains deprie Vo cuer, puis qu'il m'oublie, Que temprement m'ocie, Car trop langui longuement.	then with hands clasped I pray that your heart, since it neglects me, may kill me soon, for I have languished too long.

Douce dame jolie . . .

Guillaume de Machaut's *Douce dame jolie* ("Sweet pretty lady") is a virelai, another of the *formes fixes*. Each strophe of the virelai follows the pattern AbbaA. The refrain, in other words, is sung at the beginning and end of each strophe. Virelais are typically set in a syllabic fashion. About three-fourths of Machaut's 33 virelais have come down to us as monophonic works, though this does not preclude the possibility that other voices were added, either as accompaniment or in the form of improvised counterpoint. Virelais, like all songs of this period, could also be performed instrumentally, without any text at all.

RELATION OF TEXT AND MUSICAL STRUCTURE IN MACAHUT'S VIRELAI *DOUCE DAME JOLIE*	
RHYME SCHEME	MUSICAL STRUCTURE
A (refrain)	A
b	B, first ending (*ouvert*)
b	B, second ending (*clos*)
a	A
A (refrain)	A

Performance notes: The notated sources of this music transmit only the melodic line with its text. The performance here is purely vocal; other performance options might be on a solo instrument like the rebec without any voice at all; with voice and instrument, with the instrument doubling the vocal line; or with voice and an instrumental providing a contrasting accompanimental line. In this performance, only the first of the three strophes is sung, ending with the refrain.

22 Guillaume de Machaut: Rondeau **Ma fin est mon commencement** (ca. 1350–1360?)

((•• Listen

CD1   Track 26
mysearchlab (with scrolling translation)
Book p. 82

23 Solage (fl. late 14th century):
Virelai **Joieux de cuer**
(late 14th century)

(((•—Listen
CD2   Track 1
mysearchlab (with scrolling translation)
Book p. 83

O.L. 238

Ma fin est mon commencement	My end is my beginning
Et mon commencement ma fin.	and my beginning my end.
Et teneure vraiement.	And holds indeed.
Ma fin est mon commencement.	My end is my beginning.
Mes tiers chans trois fois seulement	My third part three times only
Se retrogardę et einsi fin.	is retrograde and ends thus.
Ma fin est mon commencement	My end is my beginning
Et mon commencement ma fin.	and my beginning my end.

The rondeau (plural: rondeaux) consists of eight lines of text set to music following the scheme *ABaAabAB*. Guillaume de Machaut's rondeau *Ma fin est mon commencement* ("My End is My Beginning") is a particularly ingenious application of the form. The cantus (the highest voice) and the tenor—in a direct musical representation of the text—are exact retrogrades of each other. In other words, the cantus line, sung backwards from end to the beginning, is exactly the same as what the tenor sings forward from beginning to end. The contratenor line, in turn, reverses itself at midpoint: it moves forward from m. 1 to the cadence at m. 20, then retraces its steps backward from m. 21 to the end. The idea that beginnings and endings are one in the same is deeply rooted in Christian theology, which holds that every birth entails a death, which in turn marks the beginning of another birth, into eternal life.

es- -toy-
pen- -soy- -e

quant je sen- toie vos- tre tres douce a- -lay-
tres- play- sant flour, dou- ce ro- se mon- day-

-ne, et vo- gent corps, ma da- -me
-ne, gar- -de d'a- mours qui mon cuer

so- -ve- -rai- -ne, qu'en- tre mes
trait et mai- -ne- -au- -tre plai-

bras si dou- -ce- -ment te- -noy-
-sir au mon- -de ne vou- -loi-

1:03

-e. 2. Je croy qu'on-ques cre- -a- -tu- re hu-
-e. 3. car sanz dou -lour et sanz pen-se- e

O.L. 238

O.L. 238

O.L. 238

1. Joieux de cuer en seumellant estoye
Quant je sentoie vostre tres douce alayne
Et vo gent corps, ma dame soveraine,
Qu'entre mes bras si doucement tenoye.
2. Je croy qu'onques creature humaine
N'eut tel bien, certes, come j'avoie,
3. Car sanz doulour et sanz pensee vaine
Mon cuer estoyt rempli de toute joye.
4. Et a bon droit, quar, quant a vous pensoye,
Tres playsant flour, douce rose mondayne,
Garde d'amours qui mon cuer trait et maine,
Autre plaisir au monde ne vouloie.
5. Joieux de cuer en seumellant estoye
Quant je sentoie vostre tres douce alayne
Et vo gent corps, ma dame soveraine,
Qu'entre mes bras si doucement tenoye.

1. In my dreams I was glad at heart,
when I felt your sweet breath
and your fair body, sovereign lady,
which I held gently in my arms.
2. I am sure that no living person
ever enjoyed such pleasure as I did,
3. for, without sadness and without any wanton
thought, my heart was filled with perfect joy.
4. And rightly so, for, thinking of you
most pleasant flower, fairest of roses, haven of
love which draws and attracts my heart, I would
not wish for any other pleasure in the world.
5. In my dreams I was glad at heart,
when I felt your sweet breath
and your fair body, sovereign lady,
which I held gently in my arms.

This polyphonic virelai exemplifies the sophisticated part-writing found in the *ars subtilior* chanson repertory of the late 14th century. In the work's sole source, the Chantilly Codex, only the cantus voice is texted. It is certainly the most melodic of the four parts and the one with the widest range, spanning the interval of an eleventh at one point in a relatively short time (m. 5–10), but the other voices weave themselves around it and around each other in an astonishingly intricate manner so that in the end each voice seems to carry equal weight, even as each goes its own way with its own distinctive melodic ideas.

24 Francesco Landini (ca. 1325–1397): Listen
Ballata **Ecco la primavera**
(second half of 14th century)

CD2 Track 2
mysearchlab (with scrolling translation)
Book p. 84

Ecco la primavera
che 'l cor fa rallegrare;
temp'è da 'nnamorare
e star con lieta cera.

No' vegiam l'aria e 'l tempo
che pur chiama allegreça;
in questo vago tempo
ogni cosa ha vagheça.

L'erbe con gran frescheça
e fior' coprono i prati;
e gli alberi adornati
sono in simil manera.

The time of Spring has come
which makes the heart rejoice;
it's time to fall in love
and to be of good cheer.

We see the air and weather
bringing about gladness;
in this lovely time
every thing has loveliness.

The meadows with fresh grass
and with flowers are covered;
and the trees are adorned
in a similar manner.

The Italian ballata (plural: ballate) of the 14th century is formally similar to the French virelai of the same period (not, as one might expect, to the ballade). The poetic form of the ballata is AbbaA, with a refrain framing the internal lines of each strophe. Most ballate have three strophes, but some have only one; most are polyphonic (usually for two or three voices), but there are a few monophonic ones as well.

Landini's *Ecco la primavera* ("Behold, Spring"), for two voices, exemplifies the ballata genre. It features smooth melodic lines that project the text syllabically, though not all ballate are quite this syllabic. The openings of the first and second section of the music are said to "rhyme," in that they share certain features of rhythm and melody, as do the corresponding cadential measures of the two sections. This kind of musical rhyme can be found in many ballate.

25 Jacopo da Bologna
(fl. 1340–1360): Madrigal **Non al
suo amante** (ca. 1340–1360)

((•—Listen
CD2   Track 3
mysearchlab (with scrolling translation)
Book p. 85

Non al suo amante più Diana piacque
Quando per tal ventura tutta nuda
La vide in mezzo de le gelide acque.

Ch'a me la pastorella alpestra e cruda,
Posta a bagnar un leggiadretto velo
Ch'a l'aura il vago e biondo capel chiuda.

Tal che mi fece quando gli arde'l cielo,
Tutto tremar d'un amoroso gielo.
   —Francesco Petrarca (1304–1374)

When all unclad, within the waters cool
By chance he saw here, Diana did not please
Her lover more than now, when in a pool
Washing her dainy veil that from the breeze
Confines her golden locks that roam at will,
This creature wild doth on my fancy size,
Until, though heaven glows with warmth, I still
Do freeze and tremble with an amorous chill.
  —Adapted from *Some Love Songs of Petrarch*,
ed. and trans. William Dudley Foulke (London:
Oxford University Press, 1915).

The 14th-century Italian madrigal began as a literary form that by the 1340s had crystallized into a series of two or three strophes, each consisting of three lines, with a two-line ritornello at the very end. Musical settings of this poetry clearly reflect its textual structure. The ritornello is almost invariably set in a contrasting meter, as in Jacopo da Bologna's *Non al suo amante* ("Never to Her Lover"). Composers of madrigals often set the end (and sometimes the beginning) of individual lines to elaborate melismas. Almost all the trecento madrigal repertory is for two voices, with the upper voice the more florid of the two. Although the tenor is often texted, it lends itself equally well to instrumental performance.

Performance notes: In this performance, the lower voice is given over entirely to a citole, a plucked instrument similar to a lute but with a box-like body and wire strings.

26 Lorenzo da Firenze (d. 1372 or 1373): Caccia **A poste messe** (ca. 1350–1372)

((•• Listen
CD2   Track 4
mysearchlab (with scrolling translation)
Book p. 85

A poste messe veltri et gran mastini
"Te, te Villan te, te Baril!" Chiamando,
"Ciof, ciof, quì quì, ciof
Bracchi e segugi per boschi aizzando,

"Ecco, ecco là, ecco là!"
"Guarda, guarda quà."
"Lassa, lassa, lassa."
"O tu, o tu, o tu."
"Passa passa passa."

La cerbia uscì al grido e al l'abbaio.
Bianca lattata col collar di vaio.

A ricolta bu, bu, bu, bu, bu
bu, bu, bu, bu, bu, sanza corno,
Tatim tatim tatim tatim tatim
titon titon titon tatim tatim
tatim tatim sonava per iscorno
No no no no no.

All in their places, greyhounds, mastiffs ready,
"Hey, hey, Villán," "Hey, Hey, Baríl" . . . And shout
"Ciof, ciof . . . here . . . here . . . ciof,"
Urging brachs and bloodhounds on the outing.

"This way, that way . . . where?
Look, look, over there . . .
Slow! . . . slow! . . . slow!
Hey you . . . you . . . you . . .
Go! . . . go! . . . go! . . ."

Midst shouts and barks, the doe emerged at bay,
Milky white, with neck of spotted gray.

To rally! Bu, bu, bu, bu, bu
Bu, bu, bu, bu, bu, without the horn,
Tatim, tatim, tatim, tatim, tatim,
Titon, titon, titon, tatim, tatim,
Tatim, tatim, it sounded as in scorn . . .
No, no, no, no, no!

The *caccia* (plural: *cacce*) takes its name from the same root word as the English word "chase." Caccia texts often deal, aptly, with hunting, though they can also depict such lively scenes as fires, street vendors' cries, and the bustle of the marketplace. The music, usually for three voices, features two canonic upper parts and an independent tenor. Many (but not all) cacce conclude with a ritornello that can be monophonic, polyphonic, or canonic. Although written monophonically, the ritornello in Lorenzo da Firenze's *A poste messe* ("In their positions") can also be realized canonically.

Performance notes: Two of the three voices are here performed on instruments: the upper line on a recorder, the middle line on a cornetto, a type of wooden horn. In the canonic ritornello (notated with only a single line), the voice begins, followed by the cornetto; the recorder enters at the appropriate point as the third voice, but begins with the music notated at m. 85.

27 Johannes Ciconia (ca. 1370–1412):
Motet **Doctorum principem /
Melodia suavissima /
Vir mitis** (ca. 1410)

((•– Listen
CD2   Track 5
mysearchlab (with scrolling translation)
Book p. 85

A: *Voice I:*

1. [O] Doctorum principem super ethera
   revocant virtutum digna merita.

   Ergo vive voci detur opera,

   promat mentis fervor, intus concita.

2. O Francisce Zabarelle, gloria,
   doctor, *h*onos et lumen Patavorum,
   vive felix de tanta victoria;
   pro te virescit fama, Pat*a*vorum.

3. O Francisce Zabarelle, pabula
   parasti pastoribus armentorum,
   quibus pascant oves; grata secula

   te pro munete revocant laborum.

B: *Voice II:*

1. [O] Melodia suavissima cantemus,
   tangant voces melliflue sidera,
   concordi*e* carmen liram sonemus,
   resonet per choros pulsa cithara.

2. O Francisce Zabarelle, protector,
   imo verus pater rei publice,
   illos ad se vocat terum conditor,
   qui fortu*n*e miserentur lubrice.

3. O Francisce Zabarelle, causas
   specularis omnium creatorum;

   tuas posteri resonebunt musas
   per omnia secula seculorum.

1. The fitting merits of his deed
   extol the prince of teachers to beyond the
      skies.
   Therefore let sincerely summoned care be
      given to living voice,
   let fervour of mind show forth.

2. O Francesco Zabarella, glory,
   teacher, honour, light of Padua,
   live contented at such a triumph.
   Padua's fame will increase because of thee.

3. O Francesco Zabarella, thou hast provided
   nourishment for the shepherds of the flocks,
   on which they may graze their sheep. A
      grateful world
   proclaims thee as reward for thy labours.

1. Let us sing with sweetest melody,
   let our mellifluous voices reach the stars,
   let us sound the harmonious lyre,
   let the plucked cithara resound throughout
      the choirs.

2. O Francesco Zabarella, protector,
   yea, true father of the commonweal,
   the Maker calls unto himself
   those that have pity for fleeting misfortune.

3. O Francesco Zabarella,
   thou dost watch over the affairs of all
      creatures:
   posterity will resound thy praises
   for ever and ever.

Johannes Ciconia's *Doctorum principem / Melodia suavissima / Vir mitis* is an example of a new kind of work, the civic motet, written in praise of a particular person or place—in this case, Francesco Zabarella, an official at the court of Padua in northern Italy and Ciconia's protector and patron. The *color* of the isorhythmic tenor is stated three times (marked with "I," "II," and "III" in the score), each time in a different mensuration; thus, although the pitches of the tenor line repeat, the rhythmic pattern changes with each statement. The optional contratenor is constructed in the same way. The voice-leading—with many hockets, a relatively free treatment of dissonance (especially in the contratenor), and cadential parallel fifths—is stylistically typical of the late 14th and early 15th centuries.

Canon **Sumer is icumen in**
(ca. 1250)

((•⊐**Listen**

CD2   Track 6
mysearchlab (with scrolling translation)
Book p. 87

MIDDLE ENGLISH:

Sumer is icumen in,	Summer has come in,
Lhude sing cuccu.	Loudly sing, cuckoo!
Groweth sed and bloweth med,	Grows the seed and blooms the meadow,
And springth the wde nu.	And the woods springs anew.
Sing cuccu.	Sing, cuckoo!
Awe bleteth after lomb,	The ewe bleats after her lamb,
Lhouth after calve cu;	The cow lows after her calf;
Bulluc sterteth,	The bull jumps, the stag leaps,
bucke verteth.	Merrily sing, cuckoo!
Murie sing cuccu.	Cuckoo, cuckoo,
Cuccu, cuccu.	Well sing you, cuckoo.
Wel singes thu cuccu.	Nor stop now!
Ne swik thu naver nu.	Sing cuckoo now, sing cuckoo!
	Sing cuckoo now, sing cuckoo!

LATIN:

Perspice christicola: quae dignacio!	Behold, Christian, what dignity!
Caelicus agricola, pro vitis vicio,	The celestial farmer [God], because of the weakness of life [the vine]
Filio non parcens exposuit mortis exicio;	Did not spare his son, but exposed him to the fate of death;
Qui captivos semivivos a supplicio	He who gives life to those half-alive captives,
Vitae donat et secum coronat in coeli solio.	delivers them from punishment,
Resurrexit Dominus.	and crowns them in the heavenly throne.
	The Lord is risen.

PES:

Sing cuccu nu, Sing cuccu.	Sing cuckoo now, Sing cuckoo.
Sing cuccu, Sing cuccu nu.	Sing cuckoo, Sing cuckoo now.

The oldest known canon in Western music, this setting of the anonymous poem *Sumer is icumen in* testifies to the predilection of late medieval English composers for thirds. Believed to have been written around 1250, it consists of a *rota*—or round for two voices—that unfolds over a two-part *rondellus,* in which the two voices exchange phrases (A and B) continuously, following this scheme:

A	B	A	B
B	A	B	A

The work is preserved in a manuscript that includes both Latin and English texts; there is some debate about which is the older version of the text, but they seem in any event to be separate—this is not, in other words, a polylingual motet. The original manuscript's instructions for performing the work direct that it be "sung by four companions, but it should not be sung by fewer than three, or two at the least, in addition to those who sing the *pes*" (that is, the *rondellus* in the two lower voices).

Performance notes: The canonic writing in this work is such that it can be realized in performance in many different ways. The present recording begins with the two voices of the *pes,* followed by a single voice in the upper range throughout an entire strophe; eventually as many as four voices sing in canon above the *pes.*

29 Song **Edi be thu,
heven-queene**
(late 13th century)

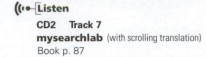

Listen
CD2   Track 7
mysearchlab (with scrolling translation)
Book p. 87

1. Edi be thu, heven-queene,
folkes froovre and engles blis,
maid unwemmed, moder cleene,
swich in world non other nis.
On thee hit is wel ethseen
of alle wimmen thu hast the pris.
Mi sweete levdi, heer mi been
and rew of me yif thi will is.

2. Thu astiye so dairewe
deleth from the derke night.
Of thee sprong a leeme newe;
al this world hit hath ilight.
Nis no maid of thine hewe,
so fair, so scheene, so rudi, so bright;
mi sweet levdi, of me thu rew
and have merci of thi knight.

3. Sprunge blostm of one roote,
th'oli gost thee rest upon;
that was for mankinnes boote
and her soul aleese for on.
Levdi milde, soft and swoot,
ich crie merci, ich am thi mon,
to honde bothen and to foot
on alle wise that ich kon.

1. Blessed be thou, queen of heaven,
people's comfort and angel's bliss,
maid unblemished, mother pure,
such as no other is in the world.
In thee it is very evident
that of all women thou hast the highest place.
My sweet lady, hear my prayer
and show pity on me if it is thy will.

2. Thou didst rise up as dawn
divides from the dark night.
From thee sprang a new sunbeam;
it has lit all this world.
There is no maid of thy complexion—
so fair, so beautiful, so ruddy, so bright;
my lady sweet, on me show pity,
and have mercy on thy knight.

3. Blossom sprung from a single root,
the Holy Ghost rested upon thee;
that was for mankind's salvation,
and to free their souls in exchange for one.
Gentle lady, soft and sweet,
I beg forgiveness, I am thy man,
both hand and foot,
in every way that I can be.

This anonymous song makes liberal use of thirds and sixths as consonant intervals. The rhythmic interpretation of this and similar songs of the 14th century is open to debate. Although the original source for this song carefully aligns the two parts, it leaves ambiguous the duration of the notes. The edition here follows the regular meters of the text, though this is only one of several possibilities. Either or both parts could be performed vocally or instrumentally.

[1] This part may also be sung.

[2] Small notes to be used only in vocal performance.

30 La quinte estampie real
(second half of 13th century)

((•⊒Listen

CD2 Track 8
mysearchlab
Book p. 89

The *estampie* (from the same root word as "stamp," as in stamping one's foot) was a type of medieval dance. Like other notated dance music of the Medieval era, it is characterized by short repeated sections called *puncta* ("points"). These modular units could be repeated, varied, and embellished at will according to the needs of the dance. In the *Quinte estampie real* ("Fifth Royal *Estampie*"), each *punctum* ("point") is repeated immediately, with a first and then a second ending comparable to the *ouvert* and *clos* of contemporary vocal forms. Here, the same pair of endings serves for all four *puncta*. Dances of this era were highly stylized, with elaborate steps executed at times by individual couples, at times by large groups dancing as a unit. The round dance is an example of the latter category: it called for a group of dancers to hold hands and move in a circle with lively stepping. Dancing was a social activity practiced at all levels of society, from the nobles of the royal courts to the lowliest peasants.

Performance notes: Medieval dances could be (and by all accounts were) performed on almost any combination of instruments. In this recording, we hear two recorders and a *bendir*, a medieval counterpart of today's snare drum, with strings stretched beneath the drumhead to create a slight rattling sound on impact.

31 John Dunstable (ca. 1390–1453): ((•● Listen

Motet **Quam pulchra es**

(ca. 1410–1430)

CD2   Track 9
mysearchlab (with scrolling translation)
Book p. 109

Quam pulchra es et quam decora,
carissima in deliciis.
Statura tua assimilata est palme,
et ubera tua botris.
Caput tuum ut Carmelus,
collum tuum sicut turris eburnea.
Veni, dilecte mi,
egrediamur in agrum,
et videamus si flores fructus parturierunt,
si floruerunt mala Punica.
Ibi dabo tibi ubera mea.
Alleluia.

How fair and pleasant you are,
O loved one in delights.
You are stately as a plam tree,
and your breasts are like its clusters.
Your head crowns you like Carmel:
your neck is like an ivory tower.
Come, my beloved,
let us go forth into the fields,
and see whether the grape blossoms have opened
and the pomegranates are in bloom
There I will give you my love.
Alleluia.

—The Song of Solomon 7:6–12

—Adapted from the Revised Standard Version
of the Bible

Dunstable's *Quam pulchra es* ("How fair you are"), a motet written sometime before 1430 on a text from the Song of Solomon, illustrates the panconsonant style associated in the early 15th century with the *contenance anglosie* (the "English guise"). Its three voices are of more or less equal weight; none of them derives from preexistent material. They all have the same rhythmic profile and they combine repeatedly to form triads that move in blocks, almost like a chorale or hymn. The intervals resulting from the interrelationship of the three voices are overwhelmingly consonant: dissonances, such as the E in the uppermost voice in m. 2, are few in number and rhythmically brief. The texture here is similar to that of the polyphonic conductus, yet the rhythms and vertical alignment of sonorities clearly distinguish Dunstable's motet from that earlier form.

Guillaume Du Fay (1397–1474):

Conditor alme siderum
(ca. 1430?)

(••)**Listen**

CD2   Track 10
mysearchlab (with scrolling translation)
Book p. 109

1. Con - di - tor al - me si - de - rum, Ae - ter - na lux cre - den - ti - um,
3. Ver - gen - te mun - di ve - spe - re U - ti spon - sus de tha - la - mo
5. Te de - pre - ca - mur a - gi - e Ven - tu - re iu - dex sae - cu - li

Chri - ste, re - dem - ptor om - ni - um Ex - au - di pre - ces sup - pli - cum.
E - gres - sus ho - ne - stis - si - ma Vir - gi - nis ma - tris clau - su - la:
Con - ser - va nos in tem - po - re Ho - stis a te - lo per - ti - di.

[Superius]

2. Qui   con - do - lens in te - ri - tu Mor - tis per -
4. Cu   jus for - ti po - ten - ti - ae Ge - nu cur -
6. Laus,   ho - nor, vir - tus, glo - ri - a De - o pa -

Bourdon

2. Qui   con - do - lens in te - ri - tu Mor - tis per -
4. Cu   jus for - ti po - ten - ti - ae Ge - nu cur -
6. Laus,   ho - nor, vir - tus, glo - ri - a De - o pa -

Tenor

Qui condolens

i - re sae - cu - lum, Sol - va - sti num - dum lan - gui -
van - tur om - ni - a Coe - le - sti - a, ter - rae - stri -
tri et fi - li - o San - cto si - mul pa - ra - cli -

i - re sae - cu - lum, Sol - va - sti mun - dum lan - gui -
van - tur om - ni - a Coe - le - sti - a, ter - re - stri -
tri et fi - li - o San - cto si - mul pa - ra - cli -

dum, Do - nans re - is re - me - di - um.
a, Nu - tu fa - ten - tur sub - di - ta.
to In sae - cu - lo - rum sae - cu - la.

dum, Do - nans re - is re - me - di - um.
a, Nu - tu fa - ten - tur sub - di - ta.
to In sae - cu - lo - rum sae - cu - la.

A - men.

Conditor alme siderum,	Creator of the stars of night,
Aeterna lux credentium,	Thy people's everlasting light,
Christe, redemptor omnium	Jesu, Redeemer, save us all,
Exaudi preces supplicum.	and hear Thy servants when they call.
Qui condolens in teritu	Thou, grieving that the ancient curse
Mortis perire saeculum,	should doom to death a universe,
Solvasti mundum languidum,	hast found the medicine, full of grace,
Donans reis remedium.	to save and heal a ruined race.
Vergente mundi vespere	Thou camest, the Bridegroom of the Bride,
Uti sponsus de thalamo	as drew the world to evening tide,
Egressus honestissima	proceeding from a virgin shrine,
Virginis matris clausula:	the spotless Victim all divine.
Cujus forti potentiae	At whose dread Name, majestic now,
Genu curvantur omnia	all knees must bend, all hearts must bow;
Coelestia, terraestria,	and things celestial Thee shall own,
Nutu fatentur subdita.	and things terrestrial Lord alone.
Te deprecamur agie	O Thou whose coming is with dread,
Venture iudex saeculi	to judge and doom the quick and dead,
Conserva nos in tempore	preserve us, while we dwell below,
Hostis a telo pertidi.	from every insult of the foe.
Laus, honor, virtus, gloria	To God the Father, God the Son,
Deo patri et filio	and God the Spirit, Three in One,
Sancto simul paraclito	laud, honor, might, and glory be,
In saeculorum saecula. Amen.	from age to age eternally. Amen.

Du Fay was an important figure in the development of fauxbourdon, a compositional technique that emerged around 1430. A fauxbourdon is an unnotated line that runs parallel to the uppermost of two notated lines, usually at the interval of a fourth below. The resulting harmonic texture is rich in thirds and sixths. The Advent hymn *Conditor alme siderum* ("Bountiful creator of the stars") alternates between plainchant (in the odd-numbered strophes) and three-voiced polyphony. In the polyphonic sections, the two higher voices sing a rhythmically patterned and slightly embellished version of the original plainchant. Interestingly, the earliest preserved version of this work transmits the plainchant melody in mensural notation, bringing it into alignment with the rhythm of the alternating polyphony. This source also transcribes only one of the two upper voices in the polyphonic sections, the "bourdon." The third voice is indicated simply by the word *fauxbourdon* ("false bourdon") written in the margin.

33 Guillaume Du Fay: Motet
Nuper rosarum flores (1436)

((••—**Listen**
CD2 **Track 11**
mysearchlab (with scrolling translation)
Book p. 110

Nuper rosarum flores
Ex dono pontificis
Hieme licet horrida,
Tibi, virgo coelica,
Pie et sancte deditum
Grandis templum machinae
Condecorarunt perpetim.

Recently roses [came]
as a gift of the Pope,
although in cruel winter,
to you, heavenly Virgin.
Dutifully and blessedly is dedicated
[to you] a temple of magnificent design.
May they together be perpetual ornaments.

Hodie vicarius
Jesu Christi et Petri
Successor EUGENIUS
Hoc idem amplissimum
Sacris templum manibus
Sanctisque liquoribus
Consecrare dignatus est.

Today the Vicar
of Jesus Christ and Peter's
successor, Eugenius,
this same most spacious
sacred temple with his hands
and with holy waters
he is worthy to consecrate.

Igitur, alma parens,
Nati tui et filia,
Virgo decus virginum,
Tuus te FLORENTIAE
Devotus orat populus,
Ut qui mente et corpore
Mundo quicquam exoravit,

Therefore, gracious mother
and daughter of your offspring,
Virgin, ornament of virgins,
your, Florence's, people
devoutly pray
so that together with all mankind,
with mind and body, their
entreaties may move you.

Oratione tua
Cruciatus et meritis
Tui secundum carnem
Nati domini sui
Grata beneficia
Veniamque reatum
Accipere mereatur.
Amen.

Through your prayer,
your anguish and merits,
may [the people] deserve to
receive of the Lord,
born of you according to the flesh,
the benefits of grace
and the remission of sins.
Amen.

—Translation by William Bowen

The new sonority characteristic of Renaissance style coexisted for a time with traditional approaches to musical structure. Indeed, some of Du Fay's most significant early works are organized according to the medieval technique of isorhythm even as they explore new sonorities. The motet *Nuper rosarum flores* ("The Rose Blossoms"), written for the consecration of the newly completed dome of the Cathedral in Florence on 25 March 1436, provides a revealing example of this mixing of old and new.

The *cantus firmus*—the term composers of the time were now using for the "fixed melody" that served as the basis of a composition—derives from the opening of the Introit *Terribilis est locus iste* ("Awesome is this place"), a chant employed (appropriately enough) in ceremonies for the dedication of a new church. Du Fay applies the *cantus firmus* in an unusual way here, stating it canonically in two voices, beginning in m. 29. The melody in the tenor II line is stated a fifth above the melody in the tenor, and each voice is based on a different isorhythm, so that the two voices move at different speeds.

In spite of its archaic isometric structure, the sonorities of *Nuper rosarum flores* are decidedly progressive. The music is full of what would now be called root position triads. The lowest line of Du Fay's motet is not always the basis—or root—of the harmony, but the lowest-sounding voice usually is, whether it occurs in the tenor, tenor II, or motetus part. Thus the lowest-sounding voice consistently provides the root of the triad sounding above it.

Even the sections for only two voices exhibit a sonority quite different from that of earlier music. In the two-voiced Italian caccia of the 14th century, for example, parallel seconds, fourths, fifths, sevenths, and octaves predominate. The most common intervals in the duo sections in Du Fay's work, in comparison, are thirds, sixths, and tenths, and each voice maintains its own distinct melodic profile.

The sections featuring four voices—that is, those sections containing the double cantus firmus in the tenor and tenor II lines—follow the outline of a consistent harmonic progression, moving from the principal tonal center (on G, sounded nine times within each return of the double cantus firmus) to a fifth higher (on D, sounded six times) and then to a minor third above the tonal center (on B♭). Although it would be anachronistic to speak in terms of a harmonic progression here—like their medieval counterparts, Renaissance composers thought of harmony as a by-product of polyphonic voice-leading—this kind of patterned sonority would certainly have struck contemporary listeners as being quite different from the motets of the previous generation.

34 Josquin des Prez
(ca. 1450–1521): Motet
Ave Maria . . . virgo serena
(ca. 1475–1485?)

((•●Listen
CD2 Track 12
mysearchlab (with scrolling translation)
Book p. 113

Ave Maria, gratia plena:	Hail Mary, full of grace:
Dominus tecum, Virgo serena	The Lord is with you, serene virgin.

Ave cuius conceptio,	Hail, whose conception,
solemni plena gaudio,	full of solemn joy,
Caelestia, terrestria,	fills the heavens and the earth
nova replet laetitia.	with new rejoicing.

Ave cuius nativitas,	Hail, whose birth
nostra fuit solemnitas,	was our festival,
Ut lucifer lux oriens,	As the light-bearing dawn
verum solem praeveniens.	heralds the true sunrise.

Ave pia humilitas,	Hail, blessed humility,
Sine viro fecunditas,	fruitful without a man
Cuius annuciatio	whose annunciation
nostra fuit salvatio.	was our salvation.

Ave vera virginitas,	Hail, true virginity,
immaculata castitas,	immaculate chastity,
Cuius purificatio	whose purification
nostra fuit purgatio.	was our cleansing.

Ave praeclara omnibus,	Hail, foremost
angelicis virtutibus,	among all angelic virtues,
Cuius fuit assumptio,	Whose assumption was
nostra glorificatio.	our glorification.

O Mater Dei,	O Mother of God,
memento mei.	remember me.
Amen.	Amen.

This motet illustrates the growing importance of pervading imitation in the last quarter of the 15th century. By its very nature, pervading imitation requires all voices to sing essentially the same musical ideas, making all voices more or less equal in their melodic and rhythmic profiles. The resulting homogeneity of texture is a characteristic feature of much Renaissance music written from the late 15th century onward.

Josquin's motet opens with a series of imitative entries that move systematically from the highest to the lowest voice. A new theme (m. 8) enters before the bassus has finished its statement of the first idea. This new theme, in turn, is taken up by each of the other voices in succession. Yet another theme enters in the superius (m. 16), overlapping once again with the bassus. The process repeats yet again beginning in m. 23, this time beginning in the altus and overlapping with both tenor and bassus. Each of these distinctive thematic units is known as a point of imitation. Successive points of imitation and cadences of varying weight help articulate the individual sections even while moving the whole work forward.

The work does not consist entirely of points of imitation using all four voices, however. Like most Renaissance composers, Josquin is careful to provide textural variety. He differentiates each unit of the text—an opening salutation to the Virgin, five strophes in praise of the Virgin, and a closing petition, a brief prayer invoking the protection of the Virgin—through a series of contrasting textures that are sometimes imitative and sometimes not. He also uses only two voices

at certain junctures, at times playing off high against low registers. Josquin organizes *Ave Maria... virgo serena* around the structure of its text. Each strophe has its own thematic material, and each varies from the others in terms of texture, cadences, and the number of voices. The opening and closing sections feature a symmetrical use of all four voices. The five interior strophes, as we have seen, move fluidly between imitative counterpoint and a more chordal texture. The texts of the first and second strophes are closely linked—both begin with the same two words (*Ave cuius...*)—and Josquin gives them appropriately similar durations and textural settings (from duet to four voices).

THE STRUCTURE OF JOSQUIN'S *AVE MARIA. . .VIRGO SERENA*			
Text section	**Measure number**	**Texture**	**Liturgical significance of text**
Salutation *Ave Maria, gratia plena*	1–30	Pervading imitation; four voices together only at the very end	A greeting to the Virgin Mary
Strophe 1			
Ave cuius conceptio	31–54	High vs. low, followed by full chordal texture	Celebrates the Immaculate Conception of the Virgin Mary (December 8)
Strophe 2			
Ave cuius nativitas	55–77	High vs. low, followed by full imitative texture	Celebrates the birth of Christ to Mary (December 25)
Strophe 3			
Ave pia humilitas	78–93	High vs. low, non-imitative	Celebrates the archangel Gabriel's announcement to Mary that she will give birth to Christ (March 25)
Strophe 4			
Ave vera virginitas	94–110	Fully voiced, note-against-note counterpoint	Celebrates the presentation of the infant Jesus in the Temple of Jerusalem 40 days after his birth (February 2)
Strophe 5			
Ave praeclara omnibus	111–142	Four voices, pervading imitation	Celebrates the ascension of Mary into heaven (August 15)
Petition			
O Mater Dei	143–155	Four voices, note-against-note, long rhythmic values	A prayer to the Virgin Mary

The cadential structure of each individual unit is carefully calibrated. The Saluation and first strophe both end with relatively weak cadences on the interval of a third that overlap rhythmically into the following section. Cadences at the end of strophes 2–4 have no rhythmic overlap but are at the unison. The penultimate cadence, at the end of Strophe 5, is fairly strong, on the interval of a fifth, followed by a rest. The strongest of all cadences—a fifth over a sustained series of held breves—is reserved for the very end of the motet (see diagram on page 116 of the textbook).

Guillaume Du Fay: Chanson
Se la face ay pale (ca. 1435)

Listen

CD2   Track 13
mysearchlab (with scrolling translation)
Book p. 123

Se la face ay pale	If my face is pale,
La cause est amer	the cause is love,
C'est la principale	That is the principal reason,
Et tant m'est amer	And to love is so bitter
Amer, qu'en l'amer	that I want to throw myself
Me voudroye voir	into the sea;
Or scet bien de voir	Now, she knows well,
La belle à qui suis	The lady whom I serve,
Que nul bien avoir	that without her
Sans elle ne puis	I cannot be happy.
Se ay pesante malle	If I have a heavy load
De dueil a porter	of sorrow to bear,
Ceste amour est male	It is love that is so hard
Pour moy de porter	for me to bear;
Car soy deporter	For to enjoy oneself
Ne veult devouloir	Is something she does not allow,
Fors qu'a son vouloir	But that one
Obeisse, et puis	obeys her will,
Qu'elle a tel pooir	Because she has such power,
Sans elle ne puis	Without her I cannot be happy.

C'est la plus reale
Qu'on puist regarder
De s'amoure leiale
Ne me puis guarder
Fol sui de agarder
Ne faire devoir
D'amours recevoir
Fors d'elle, je cuij
Se ne veil douloir
Sans elle ne puis

It is the most regal bearing
One could ever see,
From loyal love
I cannot defend myself;
Foolish would I be
to look upon her
Without wanting to receive love
except from her, I think;
If I did not want to be sad,
Without her I cannot be happy.

Judging by its circulation in contemporary manuscripts, Du Fay's ballade *Se la face ay pale* was one of the most popular songs of its time. The tenor line of the ballade would provide the cantus firmus of Du Fay's later *Missa Se la face ay pale* (Anthology I/36).

Performance notes: The cantus in this recording is doubled by a recorder, while the tenor is doubled by a kortholt, a double-reed woodwind. The contratenor line is performed on a viol.

36 Guillaume Du Fay: **Missa Se la face ay pale:** Gloria (ca. 1450)

((•—Listen

CD2 **Track 14**
mysearchlab (with scrolling translation)
Book p. 123

II. GLORIA IN EXCELCIS DEO

Canon: Tenor ter dicitur. Primo quaelibet figura crescit in triplo, secundo in duplo, tertio ut jacet.

Du Fay's *Missa Se la face ay pale* is the first Mass setting by any composer to be based on a cantus firmus from a secular source, in this instance, the tenor of Du Fay's own ballade *Se la face ay pale* (Anthology I/35). It is also the first Mass setting in which the tenor—the line carrying the cantus firmus—is no longer the lowest voice. This second feature is of particular importance, for with the lowest voice no longer bound to the cantus firmus, composers were free to exercise a wider range of vertical sonorities—what we now think of as harmony.

The cantus firmus appears repeatedly throughout the Mass and is absent only in a few internal sections of certain movements. Du Fay wrote a verbal canon (meaning "rule" or "law") at the beginning of each movement of the Mass to indicate the rhythmic value of the cantus firmus in that movement. At the beginning of the Gloria, we read (in translation from the original Latin): "The tenor is stated three times. The first time it grows by three, the second by two, the third as set down." In other words, the tenor is sung three times in succession within the Gloria, the first time at three times the value of the notated original, the second time at twice the value (beginning with the text "Et in terra pax"), the third time at the original of the notated value (beginning with the text "Qui tollis"). (For an overview of the cantus firmus's distribution through the entire Mass, see the textbook, p. 123.)

Performance notes: The ensemble here consists of eight male singers, two to each part (superius, contratenor, tenor, bass), without instrumental doubling of any kind. While such forces may seem small to us today, we know from contemporary payroll records to singers that this kind of ensemble was quite common in the early Renaissance, even in such prominent institutions as Cambrai Cathedral.

37 Johannes Ockeghem
(ca. 1420–1496):
Missa prolationum:
Kyrie (last quarter of 15th century)

((•• Listen
CD2   Track 15
mysearchlab (with scrolling translation)
Book p. 125

Ockeghem's "Mass of the Prolations" reflects the fascination of many composers of the late 15th century with complex compositional artifice. In this Mass, Ockeghem notates only two of the work's four voices; the other two are derived from them through a series of mensuration canons. Thus, the superius and contratenor sing exactly the same pitches, but in different mensurations ("prolations"), the equivalent of modern-day time signatures. The tenor and bassus, in turn, sing their own identical pitches, but in two contrasting mensurations different yet again from those in the superius and contratenor. Thus whenever all four voices are present, so too are all four of the basic mensurations. Throughout, the upper voices are in imperfect (duple) prolation, the lower voices in perfect (triple) prolation. In the first Kyrie, the two upper voices share exactly the same sequence of pitches, but the superius line presents them in the equivalent of today's 2/4 while the contratenor moves in the equivalent of 3/4. The two lower voices, which share an altogether different melodic line, move in the equivalent of modern-day compound duple and compound triple meter (6/8 and 9/8, respectively).

The Christe is a group of alternating duets (bassus-contratenor, superius-tenor). There are two halves; the first begins on a fifth (Bb/F, determined by the written Bbs in the lower voices) and cadences up a whole step on a unison C (m. 7); a canon at the octave occupies m. 5–7. The superius-tenor pairing transposes the music up a whole step (C/G), cadencing on D (m. 14). The second half uses different contrapuntal lines; the opening interval is a third (A/C), and the cadence is on an octave C (m. 19); the canon at the octave begins already in m. 16. In this edition, the repetition transposes the music a half step higher (Bb/D) and cadences on D. (The pitches of the cadences (C, D, C, D) could to stand in for a true "canon at the second," but see below.) The second Kyrie returns to the full texture of the opening Kyrie, with canon pairs at the third (superius/contratenor, tenor/bassus), prolations that translate to 2/4, 3/4, 9/4, and 6/4, respectively (but which, unlike Kyrie I, do not maintain their metric relationships for long), and a cadence on F.

Performance notes: While some recordings interpret the Christe as described above, others present the text three times (in keeping with the traditional presentation of this brief text), concluding on the unison C (m. 19) and omitting the final transposed repetition. This reduces the octave cadences to C, D, C; but the transition to the Kyrie II is smoother, with the C taken an octave lower by the bassus.

38 Ser Felice(?) (fl. late 15th century) or Antoine Busnoys (?) (ca. 1430–1492): Chanson **Fortuna desperata** (ca. 1473–1478)

((•—Listen

CD2 Track 16
mysearchlab (with scrolling translation)
Book p. 130

Fortuna desperata

Fortuna desperata,
Iniqua e maledecta,
Che, de tal dona electa,
La fama ai denegrata.
  Fortuna desperata.

Hopeless fortune,
Unjust and cursed,
Who has defamed the reputation
Of so distinguished a lady.
  Hopeless fortune.

O morte dispiatata,
Inimica e crudele,
Che, d'alto più che stelle,
Tu l'hai cusì abassata.
  F.d.

O pitiless death,
Hostile and cruel,
Who has thus lowered one
Who was higher than the stars.
  Hopeless fortune.

Meschina e despietata,
Ben piangere posso may,
Et desiro finire
Li mei guay.

Wretched and pitiless,
Well can I cry now,
And I desire to end
My woes.

The authorship of this song is much disputed. Only one contemporary source attributes it to Busnoys; most manuscript indicate no composer's name at all; and recent scholarship suggests that it is the work of one Ser Felice, a Florentine composer of the late 15th century about whom very little is known. *Fortuna desperata* was in any case the most popular Italian song of the entire 15th century. It was transmitted in dozens of different sources in the decades after 1470 and provided the basis for some 35 known reworkings; some of these add an additional voice, while others replace one or more voices of the original. And at least some composers, including Josquin, used all three voices of the song as the basis for a setting of the Mass Ordinary (see Anthology I/39).

Missa Fortuna desperata:
Kyrie and Agnus Dei (ca. 1500?)

((•• Listen

CD1 Tracks 17–18
mysearchlab (with scrolling translation)
Book p. 130

Kyrie

Agnus Dei

Josquin's *Missa Fortuna desperata* is an example of an imitation Mass (also known as parody Mass). Unlike a cantus firmus Mass, which uses only a single line from an existing source, an imitation Mass incorporates most if not all the voices of an existing work—not just a single voice—into the fabric of the new work, or at the very least into the opening sections of key movements. The opening of the *Missa Fortuna desperata,* for example, is derived from all three voices of the chanson *Fortuna desperata* (Anthology I/38). The opening measures of the superius and bassus parts in the Kyrie of Josquin's Mass are little more than lightly embellished versions of the original chanson. Yet Josquin also makes important modifications to the existing work. He shifts the music from duple to triple meter (and back again) in the Kyrie and reworks the rhythm of the tenor voice to make it move at a slower speed—that is, to function more like a strict cantus firmus. The added fourth voice in Josquin's work—the altus—also takes the tenor of the original as its point of departure.

Josquin carries the idea of reworking multiple voices a step further in subsequent movements of the *Missa Fortuna desperata*. In the Agnus Dei I, for example, he moves the inversion (melodic mirror image) of the superius of the chanson to the bass line and augments it (increases the length of the note values) fourfold. This bizarre twist is almost certainly a musical commentary on the fickleness of the goddess Fortuna, who is forever turning her wheel, bringing down the mighty and raising the lowly in a never-ending cycle. In keeping with this symbolism, the original tenor melody, having been turned upside down, returns in its original form in the bass line of the final Agnus Dei.

40 Josquin des Prez:
Missa Pange lingua:
Kyrie, (ca. 1513–1521)

((•• Listen

CD2   Track 19
mysearchlab (with scrolling translation)
Book p. 131

79

The technique of paraphrase involves borrowing an existing melodic idea from a different work but elaborating it freely in most or all the voices of a new work. In the *Missa Pange lingua,* Josquin's last Mass, written sometime after 1513, all four voices use melodic material derived from the plainchant hymn of the same name (Anthology I/40) but often in highly embellished form, with substantial interpolations between pitches. In the opening Kyrie, the composer distributes the six phrases of the plainchant hymn across a series of corresponding points of imitation (see table below). The texture is almost entirely homogeneous: no one voice stands out rhythmically or motivically. Later movements of the Mass do not adhere so closely to the structure of the hymn; at times, in fact, the plainchant is abandoned, but it returns in its entirety in the final Agnus Dei.

DISTRIBUTION OF PHRASES FROM THE PLAINCHANT HYMN *PANGE LINGUA* IN THE KYRIE OF JOSQUIN'S *MISSA PANGE LINGUA*	
Phrase of plainchant	**Measure of Kyrie**
1 *Pange lingua…*	1
2 *Corporis mysterium…*	9
3 *Sanguinisque…*	17 (transposed); 25 (original pitch)
4 *Quem in mundi…*	35
5 *Fructus ventris…*	53
6 *Rex effudit…*	61

Josquin des Prez (?) or
Pierre de la Rue (?)
(ca. 1452–1518): Motet
Absalon, fili mi (ca. 1510?)

((•—Listen

CD2   Track 20
mysearchlab (with scrolling translation)
Book p. 135

Absalon, fili mi
quis det ut moriar pro te
fili mi, Absalon?
Non viam ultra
sed descendam in infernum plorans.

Absalom, my son
Would that I had died instead of you,
My son, Absalom?
Let me live no longer,
But descend into hell, weeping.

The motet *Absalon, fili mi* ("Absalom, my son"), ascribed to Josquin but possibly by Pierre de la Rue (ca. 1452–1518), illustrates the expressive power of the motet and at the same time reminds us of just how many questions remain to be answered about much of Renaissance music. The text is pieced together from three separate Biblical passages, each of which deals with a father's lament on the death of his son: 2 Samuel 18:33, in which King David mourns the death of Absalom; Job 7:16, in which Job mourns the death of his son; and Genesis 37:35, in which Jacob mourns the death of Joseph.

The motivation behind this patchwork text is uncertain. Some scholars believe it was written in response to the murder of Juan Borja, Duke of Gandía and eldest son of Pope Alexander VI, in June of 1497. Other scholars have pointed to the death of Emperor Maximilian I's son Philip the Fair in 1506. Still other candidates include the English princes Arthur (son of Henry VII) and Henry (son of Henry VIII), both of whom died in infancy in the early years of the 16th century.

The distribution of the voices and their notation, at least in the earliest surviving source of this work, are striking: the upper two voices carry a sign of two flats; the tenor, three; and the bass, four. All four voices, moreover, occupy an extremely low range, in keeping with the textual theme of lamentation. The bass, which in vocal literature rarely descends below the F that lies an octave-and-a-half below middle C, hits the E♭ below it many times and eventually descends to D♭ and even the B♭ below that, a full fifth below what is normally the lowest note of the range. Scholars have debated this notation for many years without reaching a consensus about what it means or how the music should be performed. It may be that the work was sung in transposition at a higher pitch. One later version of *Absalon* (from the mid-16th century) transposes the work upward by a ninth (which makes the uppermost voice difficult to sing). But if the work was meant to be transposed, why was it notated in such a low range in the first place? Surely this had something to do with the text's theme of loss and mourning. The bass hits its lowest note at the very end of the piece, on the word *plorans* ("weeping"), concluding a line set to the words *non vivam ultra, sed descendam in infernum plorans* ("Let me live no longer but descend into hell, weeping"). In an early instance of word painting—the use of musical elements to imitate the meaning of a specific passage of a text—the pain and depths of hell are represented by an unusually low pitch. Still other commentators have pointed out that the concept of fixed pitch did not exist in Josquin's time—a low F in Milan was not necessarily the same as a low F in Rome—and have suggested that the notation is effectively an instruction to the performers to sing the music as low as they possibly can.

The notation of *Absalom fili mi* also raises the vexing issue of *musica ficta* (see Focus: *Musica ficta*, textbook, p. 136). As a look at specific passages reveals, it is one thing to learn the conventions of *ficta*, quite another to apply them to a network of polyphonic voices in which changes in one melodic line frequently affect other lines as well. Consider, for example, the explicitly notated D♭ in the tenor in m. 58. This requires a flattened A in the superius to avoid an augmented fifth, which in turn demands another flattened A in the altus later in the same measure to avoid a cross-relation (the simultaneous or nearly simultaneous sounding of two pitches a half-step apart) between the A♭ in the superius and the notated A♭ in the altus. The A in the altus should remain unflattened, however, at the end of m. 59 to provide a half-step move to the cadential B♭ that follows. Matters get even more convoluted as the work progresses, as for example with the cascading consequences of the notated G♭ in m. 66 and in m. 83.

Performance notes: Like most modern recordings, the version here transposes the music to a more singable range—in this case, up a fourth, beginning on E♭ rather than B♭.

42 Guillaume Du Fay:
Chanson **Adieu ces bons vins de Lannoys**
(ca. 1425–ca. 1450)

((•• Listen
CD2   Track 21
mysearchlab (with scrolling translation)
Book p. 138

Je m'en vois tout arquant des nois,
Car je ne truis feves ne pois,
Dont bien souvent entier mennoye.
Adieu ces bons vins de Lannoys,
Adieu dames, adieu borgois,
Adieu celle que tant amoye,

De moy seres, par plusieurs fois
Regretés par dedans les bois,
Ou il n'y a sentier ne voye;
Puis ne scaray que faire doye,
Se je ne crie a haute vois.

Adieu ces bons vins de Lannoys,
Adieu dames, adieu borgois,
Adieu celle que tant amoye,
Adieu toute playsante joye,
Adieu tous compaignons galois.

I am going away aiming my bow at nuts,
For I find neither beans nor peas,
Of which very often I bore a load.
Farewell these good wines of Lannoys,
Farewell ladies, farewell citizens,
Farewell she whom I so loved.

By me you will be very often
Missed, as I go through the woods,
Where there is no path or way;
Then I shall not know what to do,
If I do not cry out aloud.

Farewell these good wines of Lannoys,
Farewell ladies, farewell citizens,
Farewell shc whom I so loved,
Farewell every pleasing joy,
Farewell all my gallant companions.

Du Fay's rondeau *Adieu ces bons vins de Lannoys* ("Farewell These Good Wines of Lannoys") illustrates the composer's early style and is typical of many chansons written between around 1425 and 1450. It opens and closes with brief untexted passages that were likely performed instrumentally. Only the uppermost line, the superius, is texted in the sources, and the tenor and contratenor were probably performed on instruments. Indeed, many Renaissance sources transmit chansons with no text at all, suggesting that this repertory might well have been performed at times entirely on instruments, with no singing at all. The three voices in this particular chanson move in more or less the same rhythms throughout, with little syncopation. The tenor and the superius are the structural voices, providing all necessary consonances at openings and cadences. The contratenor is a filler voice; it cannot substitute for either the superius or the tenor to provide needed points of consonance. And in contrast to the other two voices, which are characterized by conjunct motion, the contratenor features several octave leaps.

Adieu ces bons vins de Lannoys,
Adieu dames, adieu borgois,
Adieu celle que tant amoye,
Adieu toute playsante joye,
Adieu tous compaignons galois.

Farewell these good wines of Lannoys,
Farewell ladies, farewell citizens,
Farewell she whom I so loved,
Farewell every pleasing joy,
Farewell all my gallant companions.

43 Antoine Busnoys: Chanson

Je ne puis vivre ainsy (ca. 1470)

((•• Listen

CD3   Track 1
mysearchlab (with scrolling translation)
Book p. 139

Je ne puis vivre ainsy tousjours
Au mains que j'aye en mes dolours
Quelque confort
Une seulle heure, ou mains ou fort;
Et tous les jours
Léaument serviray Amours
Jusqu'a la mort.

Noble femme de nom et d'armes,
Escript vous ay ce dittier-cy,

Des [ieulx] plourant a chauldes larmes
Affin qu'ayés de moy merchy.

Quant a moy, je *me* meurs [bon cours],
Vellant les nuytz, faisant cent tours,
En criant fort:
"Vengance!" a Dieu, car a grant tort
Je noye en plours
Lorsqu'au besoing me fault secours—
Et Pitié dort.

Je ne puis *vivre ainsy tousjours*
Au mains que j'aye en mes dolours
Quelque confort
Une seulle heure, ou mains ou fort;
Et tous les jours
Léaument servirary Amours
Jusqu'a la mort.

I cannot live like this forever
Unless I have in my distress
Some comfort,
Just an hour, or less—or more,
And every day

Faithfully I'll serve the god of Love
Unto death.

Woman, noble in name and in arms,
I have written you this ditty

Weeping from my eyes hot tears
That you may have mercy on me.

As to me, I waste away apace,
Awake at night, walking in a hundred circles,
Crying aloud
"Vengeance!" to God, for, most unjustly,
I'm drowning in tears.
Just when I need it, I get no help,
And Pity—sleeps.

I cannot live like this forever
Unless I have in my distress
Some comfort,
Just an hour, or less—or more,
And every day
Faithfully I'll serve the god of Love
Unto death.

Antoine Busnoys' *Je ne puis vivre ainsy* is a lover's lament ("I cannot live like this forever / Unless I have in my distress / Some comfort, / Just an hour, or less—or more...."). The text forms an acrostic: the first letter of each line of the text spells out the name of the woman who has caused such anguish: Jaqueline d'Aquevile. We do not know the biographical details of who she was or on whom she inflicted such torment, but the nature of the pain is clear enough.

Busnoy's setting of this French text gives equal importance to all three voices, with a good deal of imitative counterpoint. This is typical of the chanson repertory in the later decades of the 15th century. The music follows the pattern of a virelai (ABBAA), with the text of the opening and closing "A" section—the refrain—identical both textually and musically. (A virelai consisting of a single stanza was also known in the 15th century as a *bergerette*.) The mensuration changes from triple in the A section to double in the B section, and the inflections on E♭ and B♭ in the second half of the B section are particularly effective in creating contrast with the opening A section.

44 Henricus Isaac
(ca. 1450–1517): **Innsbruck,**
ich muss dich lassen (ca. 1530)

))•⌐**Listen**
CD3 Track 2
mysearchlab (with scrolling translation)
Book p. 141

Innsbruck, ich muss dich lassen,
ich fahr dahin mein Strassen,
in fremde Land dahin.
Mein Freud is mir genommen,
die ich nit weiss bekommen
wo ich im Elend bin.

Gross Leid muss ich jetzt tragen,
das ich allein tu klagen
dem liebsten Buhlen mein.
Ach Lieb, nun lass mich Armen
im Herzen dein erbarmen,
dass ich muss dannen sein.

Mein Trost ob allen Weiben,
dein tu ich ewig bleiben,
stet treu, der Ehren fromm.
Nun muss dich Gott bewahren,
in aller Tugend sparen,
bis dass ich wiederkomm.

Innsbruck, I must leave you,
To go along my pathway
to strange and distant lands.
My joy from me has faded.
I don't know how to find it.
I am in sorrow's hands.

I am burdened with great sorrow
which I can remedy only
through the one dearest to me.
O my love, leave me not bereft
of compassion in your heart
that I must part from you.

My consolation above all other women,
I remain yours forever,
always faithful, in true honor.
And now, may God protect you,
safe in virtue,
till I return.

As in the case of Josquin, most of Isaac's surviving music was religious in nature, but, like his contemporary, Isaac wrote or arranged numerous examples of the French chanson, the Italian frottola, and the German Tenorlied (see Chapter 6, p. 162). The well-known Lied *Innsbruck, ich muss dich lassen,* is not certain to be by Isaac, but he set it twice, once with the tune in the tenor (typical of a Tenorlied) in canon with the altus, the other with the tune in the soprano, in a more Italian manner (termed a *Diskantlied*); the second version is presented here. Even then, Isaac was not finished with *Innsbruck*; it is one of several cantus firmi in his *Missa carminum.*

Even after Isaac, the tune and his settings had a long lifespan, with further arrangements by other composers, a setting to the Lutheran chorale *O Welt, ich muss dich lassen* in 1642 (which appears in Bach's Cantata BWV 97, *In allen meinen Taten,* and the *St. Matthew Passion*), and borrowings by Telemann, Liszt, Brahms, and Hugo Distler.

45 Marchetto Cara (ca. 1470–1525): (◖• Listen

Hor venduto ho la speranza
(ca. 1500–1504)

CD3 Track 3
mysearchlab (with scrolling translation)
Book p. 142

Ogni de - bit' ho pa - ga - to E an_cor cre - di - to m'a_van - za.

ut supra

Hor vendut'ho la speranza	I have sold the hope
Che sì cara la camprai	For which I paid so much.
E se ben ne ho perso assai	And if I lost badly in the bargain,
Patientia che gli è usanza.	I'll have patience, for that's the way things are.

Ogni merce vol ventura,	Every dealing carries risk,
Io fu' in questa venturato	I was unlucky in this one;
Forsi mo porrò più cura	Perhaps I shall be more careful
In ogni altro mio mercato.	In all my other dealings.
Ogni debito ho pagato	I have paid all my debts
E ancor credito m'avanza.	And still have my good credit.
Hor vendut'ho la speranza …	I have sold the hope….

Se col credito che ho anchora	If with the credit I still have
Più mi acade far contratto	I should enter into another contract
Da speranza sempre in fora	I shall always banish hope
D'ogni cosa ver a patto:	From everything I undertake;
Stato è'l mal mio per un tratto	It was my bad luck for a while there
Più appetito che ignoranza.	That my appetite was greater than my foolishness.
Hor vendut'ho la speranza …	I have sold the hope….

O insensati ciechi amanti	Oh foolish, blind lovers!
Voi che sempre stati sete	You who are always such
Di speranza gran mercanti	Grand merchants of hope,
Al consiglio mio attendete	Listen to my advice:
In speranza non spendete	Do not traffic in hope,
Ché di inganno è propria stanza.	Whose true realm is deceit.
Hor vendut'ho la speranza …	I have sold the hope….

Questi falsi desleali	These false, deceitful smiles,
Risi lachryme parole	Tears, sweet words, tender glances,
Dolci sguardi son sensali	Are brokers for those who want to sell.
De chi speme vender suole.	Now those who want to buy
Hor ne compri mo chi vole	may do so,
Ch'io per me compro costanza.	But I, for one, shall buy constancy.
Hor vendut'ho la speranza …	I have sold the hope….

Harmonic progressions in the frottola are often simple. In modern terminology, the genre makes frequent use of patterns like I–IV–V–I. The music could be performed entirely vocally, entirely by instruments, or by any of various combinations of voices and instruments. Many frottole were arranged for solo voice and lute, or for keyboard alone, for frottole were in high demand. The Venetian publisher Petrucci produced no fewer than eleven books of them between 1504 and 1514—a rate of roughly one a year.

The frottola was cultivated with greatest intensity by Italian-born composers, most notably Bartolomeo Tromboncino (ca. 1470–1535) and Marchetto Cara (ca. 1470–1525). Both were active in the northern Italian city of Mantua. Cara's *Hor venduto ho la speranza* appeared in the first book of frottole published by Petrucci in 1504 in a four-voice version and then later in a version for solo voice and lute in 1509, also published by Petrucci. The lute part of this later version, which is the one that appears in the anthology, is essentially polyphonic, in two voices.

Performance notes: Rather than sing each strophe relentlessly as written, the ensemble here takes a more creative approach to performance, beginning with a solo lute version of the refrain, followed a reiteration of the refrain by the voice with the full ensemble of lute, viols, cornetto, and drum. The individual strophes then proceed, with the return of the refrain sometimes sung, sometimes played. This kind of informal approach to the notated score is still evident in popular song of more recent times.

46 Josquin des Prez (?): **El grillo**
(ca. 1500–1505)

((•• Listen

CD3 Tracks 4/5
mysearchlab (with scrolling translation)
Book p. 144

1 El grillo è buon cantore,
2 Che tienne longo verso;
3 Dale beve grillo canta.

4 Ma non fa come gli altri uccelli,
5 Come li han cantato un poco,
6 Van' de fatto in altro loco.

7 Sempre el grillo sta pur saldo,
8 Quando la maggior è'l caldo
9 Al' hor canta sol per amore.

The cricket is a good singer
Who can hold a long line;
Give him drink and the cricket sings.

But he doesn't do what birds do:
After they've sung a bit,
They go somewhere else.

The cricket always stays put,
And when the weather is hottest,
He sings solely for love.

The musical style of this frottola contrasts sharply with that of contemporary chansons. The very title of *El grillo* ("The Cricket") tells us that we are far from the realm of courtly love in which the poetry of the chanson usually dwells. *El grillo* is predominantly chordal in texture, occasionally antiphonal (in the back-and-forth between high and low voices in m. 11–14), and not at all imitative. The authorship of the work is unclear. In the only contemporary source in which it appears—Petrucci's third book of frottole, published in Venice in 1505—it is ascribed to "Josquin d'Ascanio." This may or may not be Josquin des Prez; recent research suggests that it may have been the "other" Josquin in the service of Cardinal Ascanio Sforza of Milan from 1459–1498. Whoever wrote the piece had a wonderful knack for translating animal sounds into music, however.

Performance notes: This frottola is heard in two versions, a full rendition of the Petrucci publication, and in an interpretation by Shirley Rumsey in which she accompanies herself on lute. All the voices of the original four-part version are present—one in the voice, three in the lute—and the texture thus remains polyphonic. But the clear prominence of the voice against the lute gives the strong impression of a solo song with supporting accompaniment. True homophonic texture, notated as such, would not emerge until the years just prior to 1600, as the Baroque style was beginning to evolve. But the sound of a solo voice partnered with one or more instruments was already familiar to audiences well before this time.

47 Claudin de Sermisy
(ca. 1490–1562): Chanson
Tant que vivray
(ca. 1520–1528)

))•─Listen
CD3 **Track 6**
mysearchlab (with scrolling translation)
Book p. 154

Tant que vivray en aage florissant
Je serviray d'amours le roy puissant
En faictz, en ditz, en chansons et accordz;
Par plusieurs jours m'a tenu languissant,
Et puis après ma fait resjoyssant,
Car j'ay l'amour de la belle au gents corps;

Son alliance, c'est ma fiance
Son cœur est mien, le mien est sien,
Fy de tristesse, vive liesse,
Puisqu'en amours a tant de biens.

Quand je la veux servir et honorer
Quand par esprit veux son nom decorer
Quand je la voie et visite souvent
Ses envieux non font que murmurer,
Mais notre amour n'en saurer moins durer
Autant ou plus en emporte le vent.
Malgré envie toute ma vie
Je serviray et chanterer
C'est la première, c'est la dernière,
Que j'ay servie et serviray.

As long as I live in my prime,
I shall serve the mighty king of Love
in deeds, in words, in songs, in harmonies.
That king made me languish a while;
but afterwards he made me rejoice,
since now I have the love of the sweetbodied
    beauty.

In her friendship is my trust,
her heart is mine, mine hers.
Away with sadness, long live gladness!—
since there are so many good things in love.

When I seek to serve and honor her,
when I seek to adorn her name with my words,
when I see and visit her—
her enviers only gossip.
But our love doesn't last any less long for that;
the wind carries their gossip and more away.
Despite their envy, I shall serve her
And sing of her all my life.
She is the first, she is the last
whom I have served and shall serve.
                —Translation by Lawrence Rosenwald

Tant que vivray ("As long as I live") is a typical Parisian chanson. First published in 1528, it provided fodder for dozens of subsequent arrangements and reworkings (some with new texts) and was still being printed in anthologies more than 100 years later. Sermisy's chanson is modest in dimension, with a lyrical melody that lies squarely in the uppermost voice. The text is conventional and unpretentious, a love song in praise first of love itself, and then of the beloved. The rhythms and cadences of the music largely mirror those of the text, with one syllable per note except for a few discrete melismas toward the very ends of the phrases, as in m. 10. Except for a hint of imitation on the words *Son cueur est mien, le mien est sien* ("Her heart is mine, mine is hers") in m. 14–16, the text is declaimed in a predominantly chordal fashion.

48   Jacob Arcadelt (ca. 1505–1568):
Madrigal **Il bianco e dolce
cigno** (ca. 1535–1539)

((•–Listen

CD3   Track 7
mysearchlab (with scrolling translation)
Book p. 155

CMM 312

0:37

Il bianco e dolce cigno
cantando more et io
piangendo giung' al fin del viver mio.
Stran' e diversa sorte,
ch'ei more sconsolato
et io moro beato.
Morte che nel morire
m'empie di gioia tutto e di desire.
Se nel morir' altro dolor non sento
di mille mort' il dì sarei contento.

The white and gentle swan
dies singing, and I
weeping, approach the end of my life.
Strange and different fates,
that the swan dies disconsolate,
and I die blissful.
In dying, death
fills me wholly with joy and the object of my desire.
If in dying I feel no other pain
I would be happy to die a thousand times each day.

With its clear declamation, modest dimensions, limited use of word painting, and predominantly chordal texture, Arcadelt's *Il bianco e dolce cigno* ("The White and Gentle Swan") exemplifies the early madrigal. The text plays on two poetic conceits. One is the legend that swans, otherwise mute, sing just before they die. The other is a pun on the word death, used in one sense literally and in another as a euphemism (popular among Renaissance poets) for sexual climax. The poem's narrator contrasts the literal death of the swan, who sings yet is disconsolate, with his own desire for a euphemistic death "a thousand times a day." "Death," he explains, "fills me wholly with joy and desire."

Arcadelt's setting of this poem is at once tasteful and graphic. His music is more rhythmically supple than that of the typical frottola and he attends to the projection of individual words—the unexpected inflection on *piagendo* ("weeping") in m. 6–7, for example—without diverting the flow of the music as a whole. Toward the very end, however, on the words *di mille mort' il dì*, ("a thousand deaths a day"), he introduces a suggestively rapid-fire imitative counterpoint that resolves chordally on the words *sarei contento* ("would make me happy").

49 Cipriano de Rore (1516–1565): Madrigal **Da le belle contrade d'oriente** (1566)

 Listen
CD3 Track 8
mysearchlab (with scrolling translation)
Book p. 155

Da le belle contrade d'oriente
Chiara e lieta s'ergea Ciprigna, et io
Fruiva in braccio al divin idol mio
Quel piacer che non cape humana mente,

Quando sentii dopo un sospir ardente:
"Speranza del mio cor, dolce desio,
Te'n vai, haime, sola mi lasci, adio.
Che sarà qui di me scura e dolente?
Ahi crudo Amor, ben son dubiose e corte
Le tue dolcezze, poi ch'ancor ti godi
Che l'estremo piacer finisca in pianto."
Nè potendo dir più, cinseme forte,
Iterando gl'amplessi in tanti nodi,
Che giamai ne fer più l'edra o l'acanto.

From the lovely realms of the East
Clear and joyful rose Venus, the Morning Star, and I
Enjoyed in the arms of my divine beloved
That pleasure no human mind can grasp,

When I heard, after an ardent sigh:
"Hope of my heart, sweet desire,
You go, alas, you leave me here alone. Farewell!
What shall become of me here, sad and sorrowful?
Alas, cruel love, your pleasures are indeed
Uncertain and brief, for while I yet enjoy you,
The greatest happiness ends in tears."
Unable to say any more, she held me tightly,
Repeating the embraces in more entwinings
Than ever were made by the ivy or acanthus.

Cipriano de Rore's *Da le belle contrade d'oriente* ("From the fair region of the East") exemplifies the stylistic changes that distinguish the mid-century madrigal from earlier manifestations of the genre. The part-writing is more imitative and less chordal, and with five voices, the texture is fuller. By the 1560s, five voices had become the norm for madrigals, although works for four and even three voices continued to appear through the end of the century.

The text of Rore's madrigal, by an unknown poet, draws on the age-old image of two lovers parting at dawn. The young man describes himself as musing contentedly in the arms of his beloved when she cries out in anguish over his impending departure. She then embraces him even more tightly, so that they become entwined like ivy and acanthus vines. Rore creates a distinctive musical profile for each line or pair of lines of this text, using melodic material with more internal contrasts than did Arcadelt. Rore also devotes more attention to individual words and phrases. He articulates the anxiety in the beloved's words *sola me lasci* ("you are leaving me alone")—and mimics their meaning—by setting them in a passage that the cantus (superius) voice sings entirely alone for a full measure (33). He conveys the meaning of the phrase *iterando gl'amplessi* ("repeating her embraces") with many repetitions (from m. 62 onward). And he captures the image of acanthus entwining itself around ivy by setting the word *edra* ("ivy") to relatively slow notes and *acanto* ("acanthus") to a sinuously rapid melisma (m. 72–81).

It is easy to see why almost forty years later Claudio Monteverdi (see textbook, Chapter 8) would point specifically to this composition (among others) in defending an aesthetic in which the "harmony obeys [the] words exactly." Monteverdi considered Rore one of the true founders of what he called "modern music" precisely because of the way he shaped his compositions around the text at hand.

50 Maddalena Casulana
(ca. 1544–after 1583):
Madrigal **Morir non può
il mio cuore** (1566)

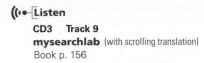

Listen

CD3 Track 9
mysearchlab (with scrolling translation)
Book p. 156

Morir non può il mio cuore,
Ucciderlo vorrei, poi che ve piace;
Ma trar non si può fuore
Dal petto vostr'ove gran tempo giace.
Et uccidendol'io come desio,
So che morreste voi morend'anch'io.

My heart cannot die,
I would like to kill it, for it would please you;
But it cannot be dragged
From your breast, where it has long lain.
And in slaying it, as I desire,
I know that you would die when I die, too.

Maddalena Casulana's *Morir non può il mio cuore* ("My heart cannot die") is another representative mid-century madrigal that also happens to be among the earliest printed vocal works by a professional woman composer. The poetic text plays on the idea of a lover "owning" the heart of his or her beloved. But the relationship here has obviously gone sour, and the imagery is quite violent. The narrator would like to drive a stake through his (or her) own heart, since it causes so much pain, "but it cannot be dragged out from your breast where it has lain for so long." The narrator also recognizes that to commit suicide would also kill the beloved. Whether this is a good thing or not remains wonderfully ambiguous.

Casulana's music projects the despairing tone of this poem in measured but effective terms. The music is sometimes contrapuntal (as in m. 1–3), sometimes chordal (as in m. 4–5). The rising chromatic progression at the end of the text on the line *so che morreste voi* ("I know that you would die"), beginning at m. 15 and repeated at m. 21, is particularly effective. The major third of the final cadence conveys the idea of death as a means of achieving peace.

51 Luca Marenzio
(1553 or 1554–1599): Madrigal
Solo e pensoso
(ca. 1595–1599)

◖◖● **Listen**
CD3 Track 10
mysearchlab (with scrolling translation)
Book p. 156

et io con lu — i, et io_con lu — i, et io con lu — i.

i, cer-car non so et io con lu — i.

me — co, et io con lu — i, et io con lu — i.

et io con lu — i, et io con lu — i, et io con lu — i.

car non so et io con lu — i, et io con lu — i.

		Starting	Textual emphasis
WORD PAINTING IN MARENZIO'S *SOLO E PENSOSO*, PART I			
Italian text	**English translation**	**Starting measure**	**Textual emphasis and musical effect**
Solo e pensoso i più deserti campi	Alone and pensive through the most deserted fields	1	Solitude and contemplation, conveyed by the isolation and extraordinary chromaticism of the uppermost voice
vo misurando a passi tardi e lenti,	I go with measured steps, dragging and slow	9	Slow steps, conveyed by long note values
e gl'occhi porto per fuggir intenti	And my eyes intently watch in order to flee	25	Running, conveyed by points of temporally close imitation
dove vestiggio human l'arena stampi.	From any spot where the trace of man the sand imprints.	33	A fixed spot, conveyed by relatively static melody and rhythm
Altro schermo non trovo che me scampi	No other defense do I find to escape	44	Escape, conveyed by the rapid imitative figure on "scampi" ("escape")
dal manifesto accorger de le genti,	From the plain knowledge of people,	56	Commonplace people and knowledge, conveyed by a relatively undistinctive passage, stated only once
perché ne gl'atti d'allegrezza spenti	Because in my actions, of joy devoid	63	The absence of joy, conveyed by a thinner texture of mostly three voices
di fuor si legge com'io dentr'avampi.	From without one may read how I blaze within.	66	The contrast between external calm and inward agitation, conveyed by the juxtaposition of slow and rapid rhythms

In the later decades of the 16th century, madrigal composers took word-painting to greater extremes than ever before. Marenzio's *Solo e pensoso* ("Alone and pondering"), set to a text by Petrarch, illustrates the lengths to which composers were willing to go to capture the meaning and emotion of a text. The opening measure is harmonically extraordinary, moving from the outline of a G major triad to one on E major, with a spectacularly exposed octave leap in the alto that reverses the motion of the previously steady downward skips. The piece proceeds to unfold in an even more bizarre fashion. The whole notes in the uppermost line that progress form G to G# in m. 1 turn out to be the beginning of a long chromatic ascent that will span a ninth (to A in m. 15) and then descend chromatically back down a fourth by m. 22.

Paratactic in form like almost every other madrigal of its time, Marenzio's *Solo e pensoso* uses musical means to emphasize key points in each line of the text. The table here spells out how this works for the first part of the madrigal. The second part of the madrigal—by this time it was common for madrigals to have multiple parts—continues in this same vein.

Seconda parte
Sì ch'io mi cred' homai che monti e piagge
e fiumi e selve sappian di che tempre
sia la mia vita, ch'é celata altrui,
ma pur sì aspre vie né si selvagge
cercar non so ch'Amor non venga sempre
ragionando con meco, et io con lui.

— Petrarch

Part Two
Yet I believe that hills and vales,
Rivers and forests know of my life and
What is hidden from others.
For no matter how arduous and wild a path
I seek, Amor always appears
Speaking to me, and I with him.

52 Luzzasco Luzzaschi
(1545–1607):
Madrigal **T'amo mia vita**
(ca. 1590?)

Listen
CD3   Track 11
mysearchlab (with scrolling translation)
Book p. 158

"T'amo mia vita," la mia cara vita
dolcemente me dice; e in questa sola
si soave parola
Par mi trasformi lietamente il core.
O voce di dolcezza e di diletto.
Prendila tosta Amore,
stampala nel mio petto,
spiri dunque per lei l'anima mia.
"T'amo mia vita," la mia vita sia.

"I love you my life," my dearest life
softly tells me; and with these
such gentle words
my heart is joyfully transformed.
O voice of sweetness and delight.
Take it soon, Love,
stamp it upon my breast
so that I may breathe only for her.
"I love you my life," be my life.

T'amo mia vita ("I love you, my life"), by Luzzasco Luzzaschi (1545–1607), illustrates another growing trend in the madrigal toward the end of the 16th century: the increasing importance of virtuosity. The florid embellishments in each of the three voices seem for the most part unconnected to the text at hand. They cannot be considered word painting, for a similar figure serves for a wide variety of individual words. The same cadential gesture, for example, appears on *parola* ("word"), *amore* ("love"), *mia* ("mine"), *core* ("heart"), and *signore* ("lady").

Although not published until 1601, the work almost certainly dates from the 1590s, if not earlier. It is part of a larger collection of "Madrigals for One, Two, or Three Sopranos" written expressly for the celebrated "Three Ladies of Ferrara," a group of extraordinarily talented singers whose performances were something of a legend throughout musical Europe. Luzzaschi's published score includes a fully written-out harpsichord accompaniment that doubles the structural pitches of the vocal parts and adds independent pitches of its own as well. By the end of the Renaissance, composers were exploring the possibilities of integrating voices and instruments to an unprecedented degree.

53 Orlande de Lassus
(1530 or 1532–1594):
Matona mia cara
(ca. 1575–1581)

Listen
CD3 Track 12
mysearchlab (with scrolling translation)
Book p. 161

Matona, mia cara,	O my good lady,
Mi follere canzon,	I want to sing a song
Cantar sotto finestra,	Below your window
Lantze buon compagnon,	Lancer good companion
Don don don, di ri di ri don don don don,	Don don don ...
Don don don, di ri di ri don don don don.	

Ti prego m'as coltare,	I beg you listen to me,
Che mi cantar de don,	Because I sing good,
E mi ti foler bene,	And I want you,
Come greco e capon,	Like a Greek wants his capon.
Don don don ...	Don don don ...

Com' andar alle cazze,	When I go to the hunting,
Cazze, cazzar con le falcon,	To the hunting with the falcon,
Mi ti portar beccazze	I bring you a woodcock
Grasse come rognon.	So fat as a kidney.
Don don don ...	Don don don ...

Si mi non saper dire	I do not know how to say
Tante belle rason,	The beautiful things;
Petrarcha mi non saper,	Petrarch I do not know,
Ne fonte d'Helicon.	Nor the fount of Helicon,
Don don don ...	Don don don ...

Si ti mi foler bene,	But if you love me,
Mi non esser poltron,	I am not a fool,
Mi ficcar tutta notte,	I make love all night,
Urtar, urtar come monton,	Pushing like a ram.
Don don don ...	Don don don ...

Lassus's *Matona mia cara* ("My dear lady") offers a witty example of the *villanella*, a lighter type of polyphonic song in a homophonic style, often in dialect. This particular song is a *todesca*, a German soldier's song that like others of its kind pokes fun at the heavy accent of a German mercenary. In this instance, the German soldier is serenading a young woman in broken Italian. The text is difficult to translate into English because it derives much of its humor from the way the German accent mangles the Italian, such as the tendency to pronounce a "v" at the beginning of a word as if it were an "f." The text also lampoons the more universal tendency of all speakers struggling with a foreign language to limit themselves to the infinitive form of verbs, no matter what the context. Thus the opening line, translated into a correspondingly corrupted English, might read something like "My tear leddy, I vant make song under vindow…" And like many songs of this lighter variety, *Matona mia cara* is full of nonsense syllables that can be heard as either meaningless or suggestive, depending upon the listener's perspective ("Lancer makes good companion. Don, don, don, diri diri don…"). When Lassus's lancer pleads toward the end that he "knows no Petrarch," we recognize that we are dealing here with what might be called an anti-madrigal, one that intentionally adopts a low-brow approach to its poetry. The music, too, is less intricate than what we find in the madrigals that Lassus otherwise wrote by the dozens. Yet *Matona mia cara,* and the hundreds of other works like it, are nonetheless marvelously compelling.

54 Ludwig Senfl
(ca. 1486–1542 or 1543):
Zwischen Berg und tiefem Tal (ca. 1530–1534)

((•• Listen
CD3   Track 13
mysearchlab (with scrolling translation)
Book p. 162

The most prominent varieties of song in 16th-century Germany were the *Lied* ("song") and *Tenorlied* ("tenor song"). The *Tenorlied* was so called because it typically incorporated a well-known tune in the tenor or other voice, making it, in effect, a secular cantus firmus genre. In Ludwig Senfl's *Zwischen Berg und tiefem Tal* ("Between the mountain and the deep valley"), the popular melody lies in the slower-moving tenor. In this setting, the two upper and lower voices constitute contrasting units, with the discantus and altus moving at a faster speed than the tenor and bass.

Performance notes: Emphasizing the inherent contrast between the upper and lower voices, this performance presents the former on instruments (treble viol and lute), the latter with voices.

Zwischen Berg und tiefem Tal	Between the mountain and the deep valley
Da leit ein freie Straßen.	There lies an open road.
Wer seinen Buehlen nit haben mag,	Whoever doesn't want to keep his love
Der mueß ihn fahren lassen.	Must let that love go.
Fahr' hin, fahr' hin, du hast die Wahl,	Go on, go on! You have the choice.
ich kann mich dein wohl massen.	I can well tell what you're up to.
Im Jahr sind noch viel langer Tag,	There's many a long day left in the year,
Glück is in allen Gassen.	Good fortune can be found in every alley.

55

Luis Milán (ca. 1500–after 1561): 🔊 Listen

Al amor quiero vencer (1536)

CD3 Track 14
mysearchlab (with scrolling translation)
Book p. 162

A. Molto Lento

B. Allegro Moderato

1. Al a— mor quie— ro ven— cer mas quien po—
4. Quien tu— vies— se tal po— der mas quien po—

dra. Qu'e—lla con su gran po—
dra.

der ven— ci— do me ha.

Fine

gran po— der ven— ci— do me a.
2. Al a— mor que— rri— a ven—
3. Por po— der me— jor que—

Fine

cer y con bien ser del ven—ci— do.
rer pa— ra ser me— jor que--ri— do.

D.C. al Fine

D.C. al Fine

Al amor quiero vencer
mas quien podrá?
Quella con su gran poder
vencido me ha.
Al amor querria vencer
y con bien ser del vencido,
por poder mejor querer,
para ser mejor querido.
Quien tuviesse tal poder,
mas quien podrá?
Quella con su gran poder
vencido me ha.

I wish to conquer Love
But how can it be done?
She has overcome me
with her great power.
I wish to overcome Love
and to be overcome,
To love better
And be better loved.
Oh! to have such power!
But whoever could?
She has overcome me
with her great power.

—Translation by Nicki Kennedy

The principal genre of Spanish song in the Renaissance was the *villancico*. The term was first used in the late 15th century to identify a poetic form equivalent to the French virelai (AbbaA). The Spanish composer Luis Milán published twelve *villancicos* in his *El Maestro* (Valencia, 1536), a large collection of works for solo vihuela—a guitar-like instrument with five to seven courses of gut strings tuned in the same manner as a lute—and for voice and vihuela. Within this collection, Milán presents two different versions of *Al amor quiero vencer* ("I want to conquer love"). In the first of these (Anthology I/53A), notated in simple, note-against-note fashion, Milán asks the singer to embellish his or her part. In the second (Anthology I/53B), the vihuela line is written out in a more elaborate form, and here the composer asks the instrumentalist *not* to embellish. In either fashion, the texture of this and other villancicos in Milán's collection is similar to that of the frottola: the uppermost voice dominates while the lower voices fill out the polyphonic framework.

El Maestro is important not only as the first collection of printed music for the vihuela, but also as the first publication of any kind to indicate performance tempos. Milán uses markings in Italian that range from *Molto Lento* to *Molto Allegro*.

Performance notes: This recording presents only Version A.

56

Thomas Morley (1557–1602):
Madrigal **Now Is the Month
of Maying** (ca. 1595)

((•–Listen

CD3   Track 15
mysearchlab
Book p. 164

The Italian madrigal was transplanted to England first through manuscripts in the 1560s and then in a series of publications. The first of these, *Musica Transalpina* ("Music from Across the Alps"), published in 1588, was an anthology of 57 late-16th-century Italian madrigals with texts translated into English. The most notable among the composers represented were Ferrabosco, Marenzio, Palestrina, and de Monte. The English, at the time, were in the midst of an infatuation with things Italian. Shakespeare, for example, wrote a number of plays in the 1590s that are set in Italy, including *The Taming of the Shrew, The Two Gentlemen of Verona, Romeo and Juliet,* and *The Merchant of Venice.*

In 1597, the English composer Thomas Morley (1557–1602) complained that the Italian fad was preventing his compatriots from appreciating the work of English composers. He expressed disgust with "the new-fangled opinions of our countrymen who will highly esteem whatsoever cometh from beyond the seas (and specially from Italy) be it never so simple, condemning that which is done at home though it be never so excellent."

Morley, though, had an axe to grind—or more precisely, music to sell. He had already established himself as a composer of English madrigals and was eager to see the public taste move away from Italian music. He also conveniently avoided mentioning that he had based a number of his madrigals on Italian models. What's more, he adopted anglicized versions of the Italian terms *canzonetti* and *balletti* for his own lighter, dance-inspired madrigals. The *balletto Now is the Month of Maying* is from the collection of 1595. It is almost entirely chordal in texture, very much in the style of Lassus's *villanella Matona mia cara* (Anthology I/53). And perhaps almost as bawdy: the "barley break" in the last line refers to an old English game of mixed-sex tag in which the "losing" couple often wound up kissing.

57   John Farmer (ca. 1570–1605):
Madrigal **Fair Phyllis I Saw
Sitting All Alone** (1599)

((•• Listen

CD3   Track 16
mysearchlab
Book p. 165

John Farmer published a book of four-part madrigals in 1599, which included *Fair Phyllis I saw sitting all alone*. Its pastoral protagonists, the shepherdess Phyllis and her lover Amyntas, can be traced back to Virgil's *Eclogues*. Farmer takes up the numerical ("sitting all alone"), geographical ("up and down"), and active ("fell a-kissing") elements in the text in a playful and pithy that manner that makes explicit what Morley's *Now is the Month of Maying* only suggests.

58 John Dowland (1563–1626):
Lute Song **Come, Heavy
Sleep** (ca. 1590–1597)

CD3 Tracks 17–18
mysearchlab
Book p. 165

2. Come, shadow of my end, and shape of rest,
   Allied to death, child to this black-faced night,
   Come thou and charm these rebels in my breast,
   Whose waking fancies doth my mind affright.
   O come, sweet sleep, come or I die for ever;
   Come ere my last sleep come, or come never.

The lute song is essentially a strophic madrigal notated for lute and any combination of one or more voices. It flourished in England at the end of the 16th and beginning of the 17th centuries, and its chief proponent was the composer John Dowland. In practice, the uppermost voice is consistently the most melodic, though this should not exclude other arrangements that distribute voices and instruments among any of various combinations of parts. Dowland's setting of *Come, Heavy Sleep* plays on the perennial image of sleep as "the image of true death" both in its poetry and music. The long, languid arch of the cantus line conveys an almost palpable sense of fatigue in its measured rhythms and repeated downward progressions.

A note on the edition: This edition transmits the original tablature notation for lute. What look like staff lines actually correspond to the strings ("courses") of the lute. The letters indicate which finger is to be depressed on which string, and what look like the flags of eighth-, sixteenth-, and thirty-second-notes indicate the rhythms; the indicated rhythm prevails until a different one appears. Tablature continues as a notational system today in music for the guitar, ukelele, and similar plucked instruments.

Performance note: The two strophes of this song are presented here in two different recordings that reflect two common modes of performance for this kind of repertory in the late Renaissance. The first strophe features a soprano accompanied by an ensemble of viols and a lute: the counterpoint of the four individual lines is particularly clear in this realization. The second strophe features a countertenor accompanied by a solo lute that realizes as closely as possibly the remaining three voices. The song could also have been sung by four voices, with or without lute accompaniment.

59 Thomas Tallis (1505–1585): Anthem **Verily, Verily I Say Unto You** (ca. 1580?)

St. John 6, vv. 53-56.

In England, the Reformation was driven by the monarchy, beginning with Henry VIII (1491–1547, reigned 1509–1547). With the publication of the first *Book of Common Prayer* in 1549, English began to replace Latin as the language of the liturgy, but the Communion Service continued to follow the basic outline of the Mass. This permitted musicians to maintain their existing repertory by converting the texts of existing Mass settings and motets into English.

Not surprisingly, composers soon took up the challenge and opportunity to write motets in the English language. These works, which eventually came to be known as anthems, took two forms, full and verse. The full anthem is for chorus throughout. The verse anthem alternates choral passages with passages for solo voice and instrumental accompaniment.

The most outstanding composers of anthems during the 16th century were Christopher Tye (1500–1573), Thomas Tallis (1505–1585), and William Byrd (1542–1623). Tallis's *Verily, verily I say unto You* exemplifies the earliest full anthems. The declamation is almost entirely chordal except for a few cadences (m. 11, 17–18) and a bit of word painting on the rising figure that sets the phrase "…and I will raise him up" (m. 19–20).

Performance notes: Any conductor of Renaissance polyphony must face the question of how to perform the higher voice ranges of soprano and alto. Some groups assign the parts to women, others to adult males who sing in falsetto, still others to boys. There are merits and drawbacks to each solution, and much depends on the repertory in question. The Tallis Scholars, heard here, use women's voices. The group's conductor, Peter Phillips, has argued that even the most talented boy singers cannot match the high level of a professional adult singer. Those who object to this approach in this repertory do so on the grounds that women would not have been allowed to sing in church choirs in Tallis's lifetime. For an alternative approach, using boys' voices, listen to the recording of Byrd's *Sing Joyfully Unto God* (Anthology I/60).

60 William Byrd (ca. 1540–1623):
**Anthem Sing Joyfully
Unto God** (ca. 1590–1623)

1-2: S1, S2 & A2 begin G♯ᵐ, B♭ᵐ B♭ᵐ. & E♭ᵐ E♭ᵐ, respectively, in N₁2; this version might possibly represent
Byrd's original opening.

© Copyright 1983 by Stainer & Bell Ltd.

The English anthem became increasingly elaborate over the course of the 16th century, as witnessed by Byrd's *Sing Joyfully unto God*. It features the six-voice texture so characteristic of choral music in the late 16th century. In many respects, the work resembles a sacred madrigal for chorus. It is paratactic in form and through-composed with discrete but unmistakable instances of word painting. Note the rising figure on "Sing joyfully" in m. 1, for example, the long note values and octave leaps on "Sing loud" at m. 10, and the triadic, fanfare-like figure to the words "Blow the trumpet" at m. 30.

Performance notes: This recording, by the Salisbury Cathedral Choir, uses boys' voices to perform the soprano and alto parts. Boys choirs have long been an important part of English choral culture, and for many listeners, the characteristically transparent texture of the sound is inescapably associated with this repertory.

61 Giovanni Pierluigi da Palestrina (1525 or 1526–1594):
Missa Papae Marcelli: Credo (ca. 1565–1567)

((•• Listen
CD3   Track 21
mysearchlab (with scrolling translation)
Book p. 171

The Council of Trent met in three sessions (1545–1547, 1551–1552, 1562–1563) in Trento (Trent), in what is now northern Italy, to formulate doctrines of faith, revise the liturgy, and generally purge the Roman Catholic church of various practices that had accrued over many centuries. In the realm of music, the Council eliminated a number of plainchants that had been added to the liturgy since medieval times (such as the Sequence on which Josquin had based the opening of his *Ave Maria…virgo serena;* see textbook, Chapter 4). The Council further declared that the function of sacred music was to serve the text, and that the text should be clear and intelligible to listeners.

Legend has it that Palestrina's *Missa Papae Marcelli* ("Mass for Pope Marcellus") convinced the Council of Trent not to ban polyphony altogether. The story is appealing but untrue. However, participants at the Council might very well have pointed to the straightforward and nonvirtuosic text setting in at least some of Palestrina's Masses in their defense of polyphony. Through his careful control of dissonance and largely syllabic setting of text, Palestrina was able to present the Mass Ordinary in a manner that was both textually intelligible and musically satisfying. Words at beginnings of phrases stand out with special clarity, but Palestrina introduces musical variety and relieves the mostly chordal declamation of the text with discrete melismas from time to time.

Performance notes: The performance begins with the vocal soloist intoning the opening words of the Credo: *Credo in unum Deum* ("I believe in one God"). Palestrina, like many of his contemporaries, never set these words to music, assuming that during the ritual of the Mass, the celebrant would sing these words before the entrance of the chorus with the subsequent text of the Credo ("…the Father almighty").

62   Orlande de Lassus:
Motet **Cum essem parvulus** (ca. 1579)

((•—Listen
CD3   Track 22
mysearchlab (with scrolling translation)
Book p. 173

tas,   Cha - ri - tas,   Cha - ri - tas.

Cha - ri - tas,   Cha - ri - tas,   Cha - ri - tas.

- ri - tas,   Cha - ri - tas,   Cha - ri - tas.

- ri - tas,   Cha - ri - tas,   Cha - ri - tas.

- ri - tas,   Cha - ri - tas,   Cha - ri - tas.

Cha - ri - tas,   Cha - ri - tas.

Prima pars

Cum essem parvulus,
loquebar ut parvulus,
sapiebam ut parvulus,
cogitam ut parvulus.
Quando autem factus sum vir,
evacuavi quae erant parvuli.

Videmus nunc per speculum in aenigmate,
tunc autem facie ad faciem.

Seconda pars

Nunc cognosco ex parte,
tunc autem cognoscam sicut
et cognitus sum.

Nunc autem manent fides, spes, caritas,
tria haec, maior autem horum
est caritas.

Part One

When I was a child,
I spoke as a child,
I understood as a child,
I thought as a child;
but when I became a man,
I put away childish things.

We see now a riddle through a mirror
[King James: As through a glass darkly],
But then face to face.

Part Two

Now I know in part,
but then I shall know even as also
I am known.

And now abideth faith, hope, love,
these three; but the greatest of these
is love.

I Corinthians 13:11–13

The text of Lassus's *Cum essem parvulus* is Saint Paul's famous declaration from I Corinthians 13:11 ("When I was a child, I spoke as a child"). Lassus sets the opening words in the two uppermost voices; in the late 16th century these would almost invariably have been sung by boys, thereby reinforcing the meaning of the words through their sonority. *Loquebar*, in turn—"I spoke"—is intoned by the four lower voices. The effect evokes the idea of memory: the narrator is now a man, as this single word in a lower voices emphasizes. The last phrase of the opening statement—*ut parvulus* ("as a child")—returns to the boys' voices. The next verb, *sapiebam* ("I thought"), is again given to the men, "as a child" to the boys. And so on. The turning point comes with the words *quando autem factus sum vir* ("but when I became a man"). The first words of this phrase are intoned by the men alone, but on the words *factus sum vir* ("became a man") all the voices enter. The effect is striking. Even if we did not understand a word of the text, we would have a sense of having arrived at a fullness of sound here, a goal. And at the end of the text, when we are presented with the promise of seeing God face to face, the music, appropriately enough, moves from fragmented counterpoint (on the word *aenigmate*—"in riddles") to simple note-against-note counterpoint.

63   Orlande de Lassus:

Prophetiae Sibyllarum: Prologue (ca. 1550–1552)

((•—Listen

CD3   **Track 23**
mysearchlab (with scrolling translation)
Book p. 174

Car - mi - na   chro - ma - ti - co   quae   au - dis   mo - du - la - ta   te - no -

Car - mi - na   chro - ma - ti - co   quae   au - dis   mo - du - la - ta   te - no -

Car - mi - na   chro - ma - ti - co   quae   au - dis   mo - du - la - ta   te - no -

Car - mi - na   chro - ma - ti - co   quae   au - dis   mo - du - la - ta   te - no -

- re   Haec   sunt   il - la   qui - bus   nos-trae o - lim   ar - ca - na sa - lu -

re   Haec   sunt   il - la   qui - bus   nos - trae   o - lim ar - ca - na sa - lu -

re   Haec   sunt   il - la   qui - bus   nos-trae o - lim   ar - ca - na sa - lu -

re   Haec   sunt   il - la   qui - bus nos-trae o - lim   ar - ca - na sa - lu -

tis Bis se - nae in tre - pi - do, ce - ci - ne - runt, ce - ci - ne - runt   o - re Si - byl - lae.

tis Bis se - nae in tre - pi - do, ce - ci - ne - runt, ce - ci - ne - runt   o - re Si - byl - lae.

tis Bis se - nae in tre - pi - do, ce - ci - ne - runt, ce - ci - ne - runt   o - re Si - byl - lae.

tis Bis se - nae in tre - pi - do, ce - ci - ne - runt, ce - ci - ne - runt   o - re Si - byl - lae.

Carmina chromatico quae audis modulata tenore
Haec sunt illa quibus nostrae olim arcana salutis

Bis senae intrepido cecinerunt ore Sybillae.

These songs you hear, which move chromatically,
Are those of the twelve Sibyls, who long ago sang fearlessly
The mysteries of our salvation.

The Prologue to Orlande de Lassus's *Prophetiae sibyllarum* offers a good example of musical mannerism. The Sibylline Prophecies of the title are the work of 2nd-century authors apocryphally attributed to the legendary Sibyls, ancient Greek prophetesses. The texts, which purport to foretell the birth of Christ, were accepted as genuine by Saint Augustine and other early Christian thinkers, giving the Sibyls a status equal to that of Old Testament prophets. Michelangelo painted five of the Sibyls onto the ceiling of the Sistine Chapel in the Vatican in 1508–1512. The Prologue, whose text may have been written by Lassus himself, reads (in translation): "Polyphonic songs which you hear with a chromatic tenor/these are they, in which our twice-six sibyls once sang with fearless mouth the secrets of salvation."

Lassus first focuses on the "chromatic" idea, introducing a series of jarring progressions. Within the opening nine measures, he uses all 12 chromatic pitches and builds triads on 9 different roots. The piece is ostensibly in Mixolydian mode on G; in modern terminology, the work begins with a plagal (IV-I) cadence, C major to G major; proceeds through harmonies as remote as B major (V/vi), C♯ minor (♯iv), and E major (VI); returns to C major (IV); and travels through a circle of fifths to B♭ major (♭III) before finally cadencing on G major (I) at measure 9.

By straining against the boundaries of modality, the Prologue to *Prophetiae sibyllarum* not only renders 16th-century theory essentially inapplicable, but obscures any attempt by later tonal theorists to "make sense" of the voice leading. Even in the concluding eight measures, the music wavers between E and E♭ before finally cadencing on G.

64 Antonio de Cabezón
(1510–1566):
**Diferencias sobre el canto de
la Dama le demanda**
(ca. 1540–1566?)

((•• Listen
CD3   Track 25
mysearchlab
Book p. 177

Cabezón's "Variations on the Song 'The Lady Demands It'" takes as its theme the popular melody known in France as *Belle, qui tient ma vie* ("Beautiful one, who holds my life"). Cabezón presents the melody in the uppermost voice, then takes it through a series of five variations. Typically for keyboard music of the mid-16th century, the register remains fairly narrow throughout, the melody is never far from the surface, and the technical demands on the player are relatively modest. Cabezón's ability to weave new figures around this theme and change its rhythmic profile allow him to create a set of variations that build in intensity to the very end.

Andrea Gabrieli (1532 or 1533–1585): **Ricercar del duodecimo tuono** (ca. 1589)

(((•⏻Listen
CD3　Track 26
mysearchlab
Book p. 178

In Italian, *ricercare* means "to research, to seek out," and the ricercar (sometimes also spelled "recercar") of the early 16th century is a freely composed work that "seeks out" a particular mode or thematic idea. The typical ricercar of this era is full of runs and passagework. Vincenzo Capirola's *Recercar quinto* ("Fifth Ricercar"), composed probably around 1515–1520, has all the hallmarks of improvisation: a dramatic pause after the opening strokes, the gradual accumulation of speed, and the eventual transformation of passagework into more tangible thematic ideas. The end result is a sense of generative energy, with a trajectory that moves from obscurity to focus, from generalities to specifics. The rhythms and metrical patterns are typically fluid and shift repeatedly from duple to triple; indeed, the necessity of so many meter changes in the modern transcription (including several passages in 5/4) underscores just how anachronistic our current-day conceptions of meter can be for music like this.

No. 66 Gabrieli: Ricercar del duodecimo tuono

By the middle of the 16th century the genre of the ricercar had become primarily imitative; the sense of "seeking out" was now being applied to the exploration of the contrapuntal possibilities inherent in a series of themes. The *Ricercar del duodecimo tuono* by Andrea Gabrieli stands squarely in the tradition of the polyphonic ricercar. The *duodecimo tuono* ("twelfth tone") of the title corresponds to the Ionian mode on C, which happens to be the equivalent of the modern-day major scale. The work can be performed by any combination of appropriate instruments with the needed ranges—strings, winds, brass. The writing here is not idiomatic to any particular instrument or for that matter to instruments at all; with an appropriately underlaid text, the parts could just as easily be sung. The practice of writing in a manner unique to a specific instrument is something that would not emerge until the 17th century, and even then only gradually.

Performance notes: The group performing here, "His Majestys Sagbutts and Cornetts," takes its memorable name from a group of the same name founded in 1516. The sackbut, as the instrument is more commonly known, was a forerunner of the trombone. Its tone is more focused than its modern counterpart, however, which makes it suitable for doubling voices in the performance of vocal music. The cornetto, heard here in the upper two voices, also produces a less aggressive sound with a softer edge than its descendant, the trumpet.

67 William Byrd: **Pavana, The Earle of Salisbury** (1613)

((•• Listen

CD3   Track 27
mysearchlab
Book p. 179

Sixteenth-century English virginal music comprises two genres primarily: the variation set, a favorite of leading composer-performers such as John Bull (ca. 1562–1628); and dance music, built on the principle of periodic phrase structure—that is, consisting of many modular units of equal length. This allows participants to execute a basic step and repeat it many times. It is only natural that the music for this kind of dancing should rest on a correspondingly modular musical construction, with small units of equal size combining to make a larger whole. In the simplest kind of periodic phrase structure, a four-measure *antecedent* phrase is followed by a four-measure *consequent* phrase; the resulting eight-measure unit may in turn be juxtaposed with another unit of eight measures to produce a piece in *binary form*. The reprises of each half can be played as often as desired and with whatever ornamentation is preferred.

William Byrd's minor-key *Pavana, The Earle of Salisbury* (from *Parthenia, or The Maydenheard of the first musicke that ever was printed for the Virginalls*) is a typical binary-form dance piece. The phrasing falls very clearly into a 4 + 4 pattern that corresponds harmonically to what we would today think of as tonic moving to dominant (mm. 1–4), followed by four measures beginning in what would now be considered the relative major (C) before cadencing on the tonic.

Praetorius's *Terpsichore* is a collection of more than 300 four- and five-part harmonizations of dance tunes popular in France at the end of the Renaissance. The melodies were transmitted to him by a French dancing master employed at a German court near the town where Praetorius lived. Like almost all dance music, the melodies consist of units of four, six, or eight measures, with much repetition. The bourrée (also spelled bouree) is lively, flowing dance in duple meter; its melodies characteristically begin with a prominent upbeat into the first measure. The volta (volte) is a vigorous "turning" dance (*voltare* means "to turn" in Italian), often in compound duple meter. Praetorius leaves matters of instrumentation to the discretion and resources of the performers.

Performance notes: At the end of the Bourrée, the performers in this recording repeat the opening binary unit. Although not indicated in the score, this kind of repetition would have been taken for granted by most performers of Praetorius' time. Literal repeats are quite common in dance music, and musicians often repeated large sections at will in order to fill up the necessary amount of time for dancing. This particular dance, moreover, calls for a return to the opening key—what we would today think of as G Major, as opposed to the G minor with which the notated music ends.

69 Giacopo Peri (1561–1633):
Dunque fra torbid' onde from
Il Canto d'Arione (1589)

((•—Listen

CD4   Track 3
mysearchlab (with scrolling translation)
Book p. 196

Arione

Dunque fra torbide onde
Gli ultimi miei sospir manderà fuore,
Ecco gentil con tuoi suavi accenti:
Raddoppia i miei tormenti;
Ahi, lacrime, ahi dolore,
Ahi morte troppo acerba e troppo dura.
Ma deh, chi,
O di Terra o di Cielo
S'a torto io mi querelo:
E s'a ragion mi doglio;
Movetevi a pietà del mio cordoglio.

Arion

Thus over troubled waters
I shall exhale my final sighs.
Gentle Echo, with your tender accents,
Redouble my torments,
O tears, O pains!
O death, too bitter and too hard!
Oh, who on the Earth or in the Sky
Would accuse me
Of a wrongful complaint?
And if I grieve with reason,
Have pity on me in my grief.

Peri's *Dunque fra torbid' onde* ("Thus over troubled waters") was part of the elaborate musical and dramatic festivities staged at the 1589 Florentine wedding of Ferdinando de' Medici, Grand Duke of Tuscany, to Christine de Lorraine, Princess of France. It draws on Greek mythology in depicting the poet Arion, who is about to be thrown into the sea by pirates. Arion sings a lament so moving that Apollo summons a dolphin to rescue him and carry him to shore. The aria *Dunque fra torbid' onde* is scored for four stringed instruments and three solo voice parts. Arion's line is labeled *parte principale* because it is clearly more important than the other two voices, which echo in response (*riposta*) to Arion's melody and words. All three voices stand out from the instrumental accompaniment by virtue of their rhythmic freedom and melodic virtuosity. In this respect, we can see Peri moving toward a texture that is homophonic—consisting, that is, of a principal melodic line with subordinate accompanying voices. Homophony is particularly well suited to the clear projection of a text in the principal melodic voice. Yet the instrumental accompaniment here consists of four-part counterpoint, and on closer inspection, it turns out that the tenor, the principal singing voice, adheres in its outline to the tenor voice of the instrumental ensemble. Even though the tenor's line is elaborately embellished, it functions structurally within the framework of traditional four-part polyphony.

Giulio Caccini (1545–1618):
Sfogava con le stelle (1602)

Listen

CD4　Track 4
mysearchlab (with scrolling translation)
Book p. 200

Sfo- ga- va con le stel- le　Un in- fer- no d'a-

mo- re　Sot- to not- tur- no cie- lo il suo do- lo- re,　E di-

cea fis- so in lo- ro:　O, o im- ma- gi- ni bel- le Del- l'i- dol

mio ch'a- do- ro, Si co- me a me mo- stra- te,

Men- tre co- sì splen- de- te La sua ra- ra bel- ta- te, Co-

sì mo- stra- ste a le- i, Men- tre co- tan- to ar- de- te, I vi- vi ar-

do- ri miei.

La fa- re- ste co'l vo- stro au- reo sem- bian- te Pie- to- sa sì, pie- to- sa sì, co- me me fa- te a- man- te. La fa- re- ste co'l

vo- stro au-reo sem- bian-te Pie- to- sa sì,   pie- to- sa sì.   co-

me me fa- - te a- man- te,   co- me me fa- -

trillo

- te a- man- te.

Monody opened up important new possibilities of performance in the early Baroque era. The soloist was now free to embellish at will, without rhythmic or motivic regard for any other melodic line. Ornamentation and pure flights of fancy unthinkable in polyphonic textures were now suddenly a very real option. All of this could help give the music an air of spontaneity in performance—what Caccini called *sprezzatura,* a certain freedom in the pace and manner of delivery, a kind of noble disregard for the meter and rhythm.

Caccini's monody *Sfogava con le stelle* ("He vented to the stars") from *Le nuove musiche* of 1602 illustrates the new practice vividly. The music, following the text, divides into two parts: the first (m. 1–11) is presented from the perspective of a narrator, who sets the scene of a lover venting his grief to the stars. The second (m. 12–57) presents the words of the lover himself, calling on the stars to convince his beloved to return his affections. The rhythms of the opening are slow and measured, and its pitches are confined to a limited range. But once the lover himself begins to declaim *O immag-ini belle/Dell'dol mio ch'adoro* ("Oh, beautiful images of the one I adore. . ."), the music rises in pitch, velocity, and intensity. Caccini emphasizes key words either by long notes (*adoro*—"adore"—m. 15–16) or by rapid passagework (*ardori*—"passions"—m. 29–30). The vocal line throughout the second half gives the impression of spontaneity, as if the singer is thinking up the words on the spot: the pace of delivery is never predictable. The underlay follows the rhythms of a person speaking, at times slow or even hesitant, at other times rushing forward in a torrent.

In Chapter 7, the Focus box on "How to Read a Figured Bass" (textbook, p. 205) includes the opening of *Sfogava con le stelle* in its original publication (*Le nuove Musiche,* 1602).

Sfogava con le stelle	He vented to the stars
Un inferno d'amore	An inferno of love
Sotto notturno cielo il suo dolore,	Under the night sky, grieving,
E dicea fisso in loro:	Saying to them:
O immagini belle	"O lovely images
Dell'idol mio ch'adoro,	Of my adored one,
Si come a me mostrate,	Just as you reveal to me,
Mentre così splendete,	By shining so brightly,
La sua rara beltate,	Her rare beauty,
Così mostraste a lei,	Show to her as well
Mentre cotanto ardete,	My intense passion,
I vivi ardori miei.	My burning love.
La fareste co'l vostro aureo sembiante	Make her, with your golden gleam,
Pietosa sì, come me fate amante.	Pity me, as you have made me love her."

Claudio Monteverdi
(1567–1643): Madrigal
Cruda Amarilli (ca. 1598–1605)

((•◦ Listen

CD4   Track 5
mysearchlab (with scrolling translation)
Book p. 208

Cruda Amarilli
che col nome ancora
d'amar, ahi lassa, amaramente insegni;
Amarilli, del candido ligustro
più candida e più bella,
ma dell'aspido sordo
e più sorda e più fera e più fugace,
poi che col dir t'offendo,
i' mi morrò tacendo.

        —B. Guarini

Cruel Amaryllis,
who with your name still
Teaches us, alas, a bitter lesson of love;
Amaryllis, whiter and more beautiful
Than the white privet blossom,
But also more stealthy than the adder
More stealthy, and wilder, and more elusive,
If in saying this I offend you
I shall go to my death in silence.

Monteverdi never claimed to have created the *seconda prattica* or "new practice." To the contrary: he identified two madrigalists of the mid-16th century—Cipriano de Rore and Adrian Willaert—as the originators this style, on the grounds that both composers had gone out of their way to make their music project the essence of the words being sung. The most serious public dispute about the *seconda prattica* in fact did not center on any collection of monodies, but rather on certain polyphonic madrigals that would later be published in Monteverdi's Fifth Book of Madrigals. The Italian composer and theorist Giovanni Maria Artusi (ca. 1540–1613) attacked Monteverdi's treatment of dissonance in these works as unacceptable, spelling out his objections in considerable detail in a pamphlet issued in 1600 entitled *L'Artusi, ovvero delle imperfettioni della moderna musica* ("The Artusi; or, On the Imperfections of Modern Music"). Artusi knew these madrigals through manuscript copies—Book 5 would not actually be published for another five years—and he took particular exception to Monteverdi's five-voiced *Cruda Amarilli* ("Cruel Amaryllis"). Artusi chastised the composer for having violated the precepts of counterpoint as set down by Zarlino. He objected to Monteverdi's practice of repeating suspended notes and of descending after a sharpened tone and rising after a flattened one, pointing specifically to the vertical dissonances in m. 12–14 of *Cruda Amarilli*. He disapproved of the cross-relations between G-F♯ and F♮ in this passage, as well as the unprepared dissonant entry of the A in the highest voice in m. 13 against the G in the bass. He also criticized the work for having more cadences in the twelfth mode (C plagal) than in the seventh mode (G authentic), the mode of its opening and closing.

Monteverdi replied with a brief manifesto of his own when his Fifth Book of Madrigals was finally published in 1605 (see textbook, p. 210). The set opens quite pointedly with *Cruda Amarilli,* the very madrigal Artusi had attacked so sharply. Two years later the composer's brother, Giulio Cesare Monteverdi (1573–ca. 1630), offered an extended gloss on this brief statement, and while this additional commentary may not have been written by Claudio himself, it was surely approved by him. In this gloss, Giulio Cesare Monteverdi argues that in the *seconda prattica* "the oration is the mistress of the harmony"—that is, that the delivery of the words, the manner of the oration, dictates the nature of the music, and not vice versa. He goes on to point out that Artusi, in his critique of *Cruda Amarilli,* had paid no attention whatsoever to the madrigal's words, "as though they had nothing to do with the music." And he reiterated Claudio Monteverdi's promise to weigh in with a longer statement justifying the *seconda prattica.* But this work never appeared—Claudio seems to have been too busy writing new music.

The Artusi-Monteverdi controversy exposes the fundamental differences in outlook between advocates of the "old" and the "new" practice. Artusi, representing the traditional approach, looks first and foremost at the construction of the music, whereas Monteverdi justifies the use of unconventional musical techniques with the assertion that words demand them.

72 Monteverdi: Madrigal
T'amo mia vita (ca. 1598–1605)

((•▪Listen

CD4 Track 6
mysearchlab (with scrolling translation)
Book p. 211

157

Monteverdi's setting of *T'amo mia vita,* published in 1605, exhibits striking differences with Luzasscho Luzasschi's setting of the same text issued only four years earlier (Anthology I/52). Thanks to the use of the solo voice, Monteverdi is able to distinguish quite clearly between the narrator's memory of the words he has heard from his beloved ("I love you, my life") and his own injunction to the god of love, Amor, to imprint these words on his heart. The madrigal begins with the remembered words themselves, sung by a solo soprano (representing the beloved's voice) and supported by basso continuo. Only with the entrance of the three lower (men's) voices do we realize that the opening line is a quotation, a memory. The effect is quite dramatic, with the contrasting perspectives represented by contrasting sonorities. When the memory returns in m. 9, it is not only the words that come back (*T'amo mia vita*), but also the beloved's voice as well, for this line is consistently given to the soprano alone in the first half of Monteverdi's setting.

Beginning in m. 40, after the narrator implores the god of love to imprint them on his heart and let his "soul breathe through them alone," Monteverdi incorporates the remembered words into the full texture of all six voices. The soprano sings exactly the same pitches as at the beginning, but her words and the sound of her voice have now been integrated into the body of the whole. Monteverdi projects the text "Let 'I love you, my life,' be my whole life" by folding the falling motive associated with the remembered words into the full texture of the music. Because it is a concertato madrigal—a work for voice and instruments that function both together and independently of one another—Monteverdi can distinguish solo passages from polyphonic ones and capture the drama of the poetry in a way that Luzasschi's wholly polyphonic setting cannot.

"T'amo mia vita," la mia cara vita
dolcemente me dice; e in questa sola
si soave parola
Par mi trasformi lietamente il core.
O voce di dolcezza e di diletto.
Prendila tosta Amore,
stampala nel mio petto,
spiri dunque per lei l'anima mia.
"T'amo mia vita," la mia vita sia.

"I love you my life," my dearest life
softly tells me; and with these
such gentle words
my heart is joyfully transformed.
O voice of sweetness and delight.
Take it soon, Love,
stamp it upon my breast
so that I may breathe only for her.
"I love you my life," be my life.

Zefiro torna e di soavi accenti (ca. 1630)

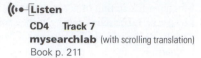

CD4 Track 7
mysearchlab (with scrolling translation)
Book p. 211

No. 73 Monteverdi: *Zefiro torna e di soavi accenti* ■ **165**

Zefiro torna e di soavi accenti
L'aer fa grato e'l piè discioglie a l'onde,

E mormorando tra le verdi fronde
Fa danzar al bel suon su'l prato i fiori,
Inghirlandato il crin Fillide e Clori
Note temprando amor care e gioconde
E da monti e da valli ime e profonde
Raddopian l'armonia gli antri canori.
Sorge più vaga in ciel l'aurora e'l sole

Sparge più luci d'or, più puro argento
Fregia di Teti il bel ceruleo manto.
Sol io per selve abbandonate e sole
L'ardor di due begli occhi e'l mio tormento.
Come vuol mia ventura hor piango, hor canto.

          —Ottavio Rinuccini

The west wind returns and with soft accents
makes the air gentle and releases swift-footed
    waves,
and murmuring among the green branches
makes the flowers dance at its lovely sound
and curls round the hair of Phyllis and Clori,
love giving rise to fond and joyful song,
and from mountains and valleys low and deep,
the sonorous caves reecho the music.
The dawn rises more lovely in the sky, and the
    sun
scatters more golden rays, and a purer silver
decorates Teti's beautiful sky blue coat.
Only I in the lonely, deserted forest—
the fire of two bright eyes is my torment.
As my fortune wills, I weep, then sing.

Monteverdi's *Zefiro torna e di soavi accenti* ("The west wind returns and with soft accents"), for two tenors and basso continuo, illustrates just how musically elaborate the concertato madrigal had become by the early 1630s. Most of the work rests upon a ground bass, a short phrase repeated over and over again in the lowest voice. This particular bass pattern, complete in two measures in modern transcription, shares no thematic material with the upper voices but instead provides a structural framework that allows the voices above it to unfold freely, without regard to their harmonic underpinnings. The ground bass also provides continuity at those moments when neither of the two tenors is singing (m. 54, 56, 58, 66, etc.). Without the basso continuo, such pauses would simply not be feasible.

    The first 11 of the poem's 14 lines are full of pastoral clichés. A gentle wind (the zephyr) blows from the west, branches murmur in the gentle breeze, nymphs dance, the sun rises in a sky of deep blue. The repeating bass reinforces the static nature of this pastoral perfection. Everything is constant and unchanging. So constant and so unchanging, in fact, that something must be about to happen. And it does: In the twelfth line, the poem shifts abruptly to the first person when the narrator says "Only I [stand] in the lonely, deserted forest—the fire of two bright eyes is my torment." The ground bass suddenly breaks off here (m. 113) and the music slows down through a change in mensuration: a breve in the opening section now equals a half note. For the last line of the poem ("As my fortune wills [it], I weep, then sing"), Monteverdi forcefully juxtaposes the contrast between joy and sorrow, setting the final statement of the word *piango* ("weep") on a suspension with a jarring dissonance (m. 143–144) whose resolution ushers in the final return of the ground bass with the word *canto* ("I sing").

74   Francesca Caccini
(1587–ca. 1640):
Lasciatemi qui solo (1618)

((⊷ Listen
CD4   Track 8
mysearchlab (with scrolling translation)
Book p. 212

Lasciatemi qui solo (author unknown; last line of each stanza echoes a line from Rinuccini's lament for the title character in *L'Arianna*, 1608)

Lasciatemi qui solo
Tornate augelli al nido
Mentre l'anim'e'l duolo
Spiro su questo lido.
Altri meco non vòglio
Ch'un freddo scoglio e'l mio
fatal martire.
Lasciatemi morire.

Dolcissime sirene,
Ch'en si pietoso canto
Radollcite mie pene
Fate soave il pianto
Movete il nuoto altronde
Togliete all'onde i crudi
sdegni e l'ire
Lasciatemi morire.

Placidissimi venti
Tornate al vostro speco
Sol miei duri lamenti
Chieggio che restin meco.
Vostri sospir non chiamo
Solingo bramò i miei dolor
finire.
Lasciatemi morire.

Felicissimi amanti
Tornate al bel diletto
Fere occh'o notanti
Fuggiti'il mesto aspetto
Sol dolcezza di morte
Apra la porte all'ultimo
languire.
Lasciatemi morire.

Avarissimi lumi
Che su'l morir versate
Amarissimi fiumi
Tard'è vostra pietate.
Già mi sento mancare
O luci avar'e tarde al mio
conforto.
Già sono e sangu'e smorto.

Leave me here alone.
Return, birds, to your nest
While I breathe out my spirit
and sorrow on this beach.
I want no other with me
But a cold rock and my fatal
suffering.
Let me die.

Sweetest sirens,
Who in such piteous song
Sweeten my pains
(And) make gentle weeping,
Move your swimming elsewhere.
Remove from the waves cruel
scorn and angers.
Let me die.

Most placid winds,
Return to your cave.
Only my harsh laments
Do I ask to remain with me.
I call not on your sighs.
Solitary, I long for my sorrow
to end.
Let me die.

Happiest lovers,
Return to sweet delight.
Fierce, observant eyes,
Flee this sad sight.
Only the sweetness of death
Opens the door to the ultimate
pleasure.
Let me die.

Greediest of eyes
That shed over my death
The bitterest of streams,
Your pity is late.
Already I feel faint.
O greedy eyes, you come too
late to comfort me.
I am already both bleeding and dying.
—Translation by Suzanne Cusick

Variation was an important structural device in a great deal of early Baroque music. This is particularly evident in Francesca Caccini's stophic monody *Lasciatemi qui solo* ("Leave me in solitude here"). The text is a lament—once again, a lover has been abandoned—that progresses from sorrow to death. The music's basic structural unit is the nine-measure pattern stated at the outset by the bass. Reinforcing the process of psychological transformation described in the text, Caccini subtly varies both the bass line and the melody in each strophe (m. 1–9, 10–19, 20–29, and 30–39, and 40–49) but maintains exactly the same music for the relentless refrain of *lasciatemi morire* ("let me die"). At the very end, however, the longedfor death is now imminent (*Già sono e sangu'e smorto*: "Already I am bloodless and pale," m. 47–48), and the slight change in the melodic line is full of meaning.

Tradimento! (1659)

((•─ Listen
CD4   Track 9
mysearchlab (with scrolling translation)
Book p. 212

Tradimento! Tradimento!

Amore e la Speranza
voglion farmi prigioniero,
e a tal segno il mal s'avanza
ch'ho scoperto ch'il Pensiero
dice d'esserne contento.

Tradimento! Tradimento!

La Speranza per legarmi
a gran cose mi lusinga.
S'io le credo, avvien che stringa
lacci sol da incatenarmi.
Mio core all'armi, all'armi!

S'incontri l'infida!
Si prenda, s'uccida!
Sù presto, è periglioso ogni momento!
Tradimento! Tradimento!
　　　　　—Giovanni Tani

Betrayal! Betrayal!

Love and Hope
Want to make me their prisoner,
And my sickness is so advanced
That I realize I am happy
Just thinking of it.

Betrayal! Betrayal!

Hope, to bind me,
Entices me with great things.
The more I believe what she says,
The tighter she ties the knots that imprison me
To arms, my heart! To arms!

Against the unfaithful one!
Take her and kill her!
Hurry, every moment is dangerous!
Betrayal! Betrayal!

Tradimento! ("Betrayal!"), an arietta for soprano and continuo by Barbara Strozzi, illustrates one of the most important of all formal innovations of the Baroque, the ritornello principle. A *ritornello* (the word means "small return" in Italian) is an opening musical idea that returns at several points over the course of a work, usually after contrasting material of some kind. Composers used the ritornello principle to establish a framework of both repetition and variation, and it appears in a great many genres of the Baroque era, vocal as well as instrumental. It would later take on special importance in the genre of the concerto.

The ritornello in Strozzi's *Tradimento!*—the exclamation "Betrayal!" and the agitated theme associated with it—is both textual and musical. In these recurring outbursts, the scorned lover swears to kill the object of her wrath. The ritornello sections offset more inward and less violent reflections: "My sickness is so advanced / That I realize I am happy just thinking of it." But these contrasting emotions are always driven out by thoughts of revenge in the guise of the ritornello ("Betrayal!").

Strozzi's ritornello captures the physical energy of the scorned lover's fury with rapid-fire repeated notes. This technique, developed by Monteverdi for evoking a mood of bellicose agitation or anger, was known as the *genere concitato*—the "agitated" or "war-like" manner. The flurry of repeated notes outlining a triad that opens *Tradimento*—and recurs with each statement of the ritornello between strophes and at the end—sounds almost like a trumpet fanfare, rousing troops for battle.

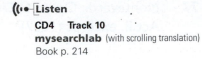

((•● Listen
CD4   Track 10
mysearchlab (with scrolling translation)
Book p. 214

(1) ♩ dans la tablature.

Enfin la beauté que j'adore
Me fait cognoistre en son retour,
Qu'elle veut que je voye encore
Ces yeux pour qui je meurs d'amour.
Mais puis que je revoy la beauté qui m'enflame,

Sortez mes desplaisirs, hostez vous de mon ame.

Le ciel voyant que son absence
M'oste tout mon contentement,
Octroye à ma persévérance
La fin de mon cruel tourment.
Mais puis que je revoy …

Mes maux changés vous en délices,
Mon cœur, arretes vos douleurs,
Amour bannissez mes supplices,
Mes yeux ne versez plus de pleurs.
Et puis que je revoy.

At last the beauty whom I adore
Lets me know upon her return
That she still wishes me to see
Those eyes for which I die of love.
But since I see again the beauty which
    consumes me,
Be gone, troubles, leave my soul.

Heaven, seeing that her absence
Deprives me of my happiness,
Grants, because of my perseverance,
The end of my cruel torment.
But since I see …

My wounds, turn yourselves into delights.
My heart, stop your aching.
Love, banish my tortures.
Eyes, shed no more tears.
And since I see …

—Translation by Ellen Hargis and Candice Smith

The most important repertory of secular song in early 17th-century France centers on the *air de cour* ("courtly air"). Like the madrigal, the *air de cour* was at first polyphonic but eventually evolved into the favored vehicle for solo voice and lute accompaniment. The first published set of this genre appeared in 1571. It includes arrangements of earlier four-part compositions as well as new works in the style of the *voix de ville* (simple strophic verse set to chordal accompaniments). Étienne Moulinié's *Enfin la beauté que j'adore* ("At last, the beauty whom I adore"), published in 1624, resembles many similar *airs de cour* in its fluid, syllabic declamation of text, and its harmonic simplicity and melodic grace, avoiding overt displays of virtuosity. Moulinié (ca. 1600–after 1669) served for many years as director of music to Gaston d'Orleans, Louis XIV's younger brother, and he was one of many French composers of the early 17th century to cultivate the *air de cour,* along with Pierre Guédron (ca. 1570–ca. 1620) and Antoine Boësset (1586–1643).

77 Monteverdi: Opera **L'Orfeo,**
Act II, excerpt (1607)

((•• Listen
CD4 Track 11
mysearchlab (with scrolling translation)
Book p. 216

CHORO

12:19

(Andante)

ORPHEUS

Vi ricorda, o boschi ombrosi
de'miei lungh'aspri tormenti,
quando i sassi ai miei lamenti
rispondean fatti pietosi?

Dite, all'hor non vi sembrai
più d'ogn'altro sconsolato?
Or fortuna ha stil cangiato
et ha volto in festa i guai.

Vissi già mesto e dolente,
Or gioisco, e quegli affanni
che sofferti ho per tant'anni
fan più caro il ben presente.

Sol per te bella Euridice,
benedico il mio tormento;
dopo il duol vie più contento
dopo il mal viè più felice.

FIRST SHEPHERD

Mira, deh mira, Orfeo
che d'ogni intorno
ride il bosco e ride il prato.
Segui pur col plettr'aurato
d'addolcir l'aria in si beato giorno.

MESSENGER

Ahi caso acerbo
Ahi fat'empio e crudele.
Ahi stelle ingiuriose,
ahi ciel avaro.

FIRST SHEPHERD

Qual suon dolente il lieto di perturba?

MESSENGER

Lassa! dunque debb'io mentre
Orfeo con sue note il ciel consola,
con le parole mie passangli il core?

THIRD SHEPHERD

Questa è Silvia gentile,
dolcissima compagna della bell'Euridice.
O quanto è in vista dolorosa!
Or che sia? Deh, sommi Dei,
Non torcete da noi benigno il guardo.

ORPHEUS

Woodland groves do ye remember,
all my cruel bitter torments,
when the rocks heard my lamenting
and in pity gave me answer?

Come reply, more broken hearted,
did ye e'er behold a lover?
Now has fortune tuned her lute strings
and has turned to joy my sorrow!

I was full of grief and sorrow,
but rejoice now in my gladness.
By so many years of sighing
is my joy today perfected.

In thy favours, fair Eurydice,
do I bless my bitter torments.
After grief is joy thrice hallow'd,
after evil good thrice blessed.

FIRST SHEPHERD

Marvel, yea marvel, Orpheus,
that all around thee
laughs the forest, laugh the meadows!
Haste thee then with plectrum of gold
to soothe the zephyrs of this blessed morning.

MESSENGER

Ah bitter sorrow!
Ah fate cruel and impious!
Ah stars of ill designing!
ah heav'n voracious!

FIRST SHEPHERD

What cries of mourning disturb this our gladness?

MESSENGER

Ah me! Wherefore must I now
while with song all the heav'n Orpheus rejoiceth
with cruel tidings rend his heart asunder?

THIRD SHEPHERD

This is Sylvia most gentle,
the sweetest of the comrades of the fair Eurydice.
Heavy her eyes with sorrow!
Whate'er her news turn not from us,
O gods in heaven above your kind regarding.

MESSENGER
Pastor, lasciate il canto,
ch'ogni nostra allegrezza in doglia è volta.

ORPHEUS
D'onde vieni? ove vai? …
Ninfa che porti?

MESSENGER
A te ne vengo, Orfeo,
messaggera infelice,
di caso più infelice e più funesto:
la tua bella Euridice…

ORPHEUS
Ohimè che odo?

MESSENGER
La tua diletta sposa è morta.

ORPHEUS
Ohimè!

MESSENGER
In un fiorito prato
con l'altre sue compagne
giva cogliendo fiori
per farne una ghirlanda a le sue chiome,
quand'angue insidioso,
ch'era fra l'erbe ascoso,
le punse un piè con velenoso dente.
Ed ecco immantinente
scolorirsi il bel viso e nei suoi lumi
sparir que lampi, ond'ella al sol fea scorno.
All'hor noi tutte
sbigottite e meste
le fummo intorno, richiamar tentando

gli spirti in lei smarriti
con l'onda fresca e con possenti carmi,
ma nulla valse, ahi lassa,
ch'ella i languidi lumi alquanto aprendo,
e te chiamando, Orfeo,
Dopo un grave sospiro,
spirò fra queste braccia; ed io rimasi
piena il cor di pietade e di spavento.

MESSENGER
Fair youth, have done with singing,
For today our rejoicing is turned to mourning.

ORPHEUS
Whence dost thou come? Whither go?
Nymph, tell thy tidings!

MESSENGER
To thee, Orpheus, I come,
cruel tidings I bear thee:
a tragedy of horror dark and grievous;
For thy lovely Eurydice…

ORPHEUS
Alas, what hear I?

MESSENGER
Thy well beloved bride is dead.

ORPHEUS
Woe's me!

MESSENGER
As through the meads she wandered
with three of her companions
gathering woodland blossoms,
Wherewith to wreath a garland for her tresses,
A treacherous serpent,
which in the grass was lurking,
Within her buried his envenom'd fangs.
And lo!
the wine-red hue of life deserts her fair visage,
and from her eyes banisheth that lustre
which made the sun ashamed,
and we, our horror and dismay withstanding,
around her stood and with cool water bathing
   her forehead,
strove to recall the ebbing spirit,
and loudly heav'n invoked,
but all in vain, ah sorrow!
For then her languid eyes
a little opening she cried upon thee
"Orpheus, my Orpheus!"
With a last deep sigh
within these arms she perish'd,
and I remained of pity and terror
a victim spellbound.

FIRST SHEPHERD
Ahi caso acerbo
ahi fat'empio e crudele.
Ahi stelle ingiuriose,
ahi ciel avaro.

SECOND SHEPHERD
A l'amara novella
rassembral'infelice un muto sasso
che per troppo dolor non può dolersi.

FIRST SHEPHERD
Ahi ben havrebbe
un cor di tigre o d'orsa
chi non sentisse del tuo mal pietate,
privo d'ogni tuo ben, misero amante.

ORPHEUS
Tu se' morta, mia vita, ed io respiro?

Tu se' da me partita

per mai più, non tornare, ed io rimango?
No, che se i versi alcuna cosa ponno,

n'andrò sicuro a più profondi abissi;
e intenerito il cor del Re de l'ombre,
meco trarrotti a riveder le stelle,

O, se ciò negherammi empio destino,
rimarrò teco in compagnia di morte,
Addio terra, cielo
e sole, addio.

CHORUS OF NYMPHS AND SHEPHERDS
Ahi caso acerbo, ahi fat'empio e crudele,
Ahi stelle ingiuriose, ahi cielo avaro.
Non si fidi uom mortale
Di ben caduco e frale,
che tosto fugge, e spesso
a gran salita
il precipizio è presso.

FIRST SHEPHERD
Ah bitter sorrow!
Ah fate cruel and impious!
Ah stars of ill designing!
Ah heav'n voracious!

SECOND SHEPHERD
At these tidings so grievous
he all unhappy stands like a rock in silence.
Grief so bitter as his no tongue can utter.

FIRST SHEPHERD
Ah, he must have a heart of bear or tiger
who would not pity feel for thy affliction,
of ev'ry joy bereft, star crossed lover!

ORPHEUS
Thou art dead, art dead my life,
and I am living?
Thou now from me art sever'd,
sever'd from me now forever.
Thou mayest return never and I shall remain?
No, No!
If there still lies virtue in my singing,
I will go down to the most deep abysses,
I will soften the heart of the king of shadows,
and I will bring thee once more to see the star
   light,
or if destiny impious this denies me,
I will remain there with thee in death abiding.
Farewell earth, farewell sky,
and sun, farewell.

CHORUS OF NYMPHS AND SHEPHERDS
Ah bitter sorrow! Ah fate cruel and impious!
Ah stars of ill designing! Ah heav'n voracious!
Bring not thy gifts O mortal,
to Fortune's transient portal;
Soon will thy goddes frustrate thee
Wheree'er thou climbest,
Lo! yawning gulfs await thee.

Having established the new style of recitative, composers now faced the challenge of integrating this manner of singing into a work that was both musically and dramatically satisfying. Claudio Monteverdi's *Orfeo* of 1607 is generally acknowledged to be the first opera to have achieved this goal. It was certainly not the first opera (as it is sometimes mistakenly called), but it was the first to gain critical acclaim. Part of its appeal lies in its keen sense of dramatic pacing, as illustrated in this extended excerpt from Act II.

Orfeo takes as its subject the most celebrated musician of ancient myth, Orpheus, whose music was so powerful that it persuaded the gods of the underworld to release Euridyce from the realm of the dead. All of Act I and the first half of Act II of *Orfeo* are very much in the pastoral spirit, depicting an idyllic world of shepherds and shepherdesses, a world without care or sorrow. Orpheus himself gives expression to this untainted state in his "Vi ricorda," a strophic aria written in a manner reminiscent of the frottola, alternating between duple and triple meters within the compound meter of 6/4. The whole is introduced by a ritornello, which reappears before every strophe.

With the entrance of the Messenger bearing news of Euridice's death (*Ahi caso acerbo*), the mood shifts suddenly. The unprepared dissonance on the middle syllable of *acerbo* ("bitter") is particularly grating. Orpheus is stunned, but Monteverdi resists depicting this with a sudden outpouring of grief, opting instead for the utterly simple but all the more moving exclamation on two long notes (*Ohimè*). The messenger's narrative illustrates the declamatory powers of the new monodic style splendidly, climbing to a registral high when it quotes Euridice's dying word: *Orfeo*.

Monteverdi also makes effective use of instrumentation here, contrasting the brightness of the strings in *Vi ricorda,* for example, with the hushed, dark sound of the *organo di legno* (a small organ with wooden pipes), which makes its first appearance with the Messenger at m. 58. The announcement of death has a distinctive sound.

Performance notes: The ensemble in this recording alters each return of the ritornello in some way, adding recorders (which play melodic embellishments) at m. 12, reducing the dynamics to *piano* in m. 23 (the dynamic markings in the score are the editor's interpretation and not in the original), and adding melodic embellishments in the violin parts in m. 34. The intervening solo passages for *Orfeo,* in turn, alter the sound of the basso continuo, substituting a harp for the harpsichord at m. 27.

78 Monteverdi: Opera
L'incoronazione di Poppea,
Act I, Scene 3, (1642 or 43)

((•• Listen
CD4   Track 12
mysearchlab
Book p. 222

Scena terza

Poppea, Nerone

Poppea, e Nerone escono al far del giorno amorosamente abbracciati, prendendo commiato l'uno dall'altro con tenerezze affettuose.

Scene III

Poppaea, Nero

Poppaea and Nero enter in the early morning light, fondly embracing, and bid farewell to one another with tender caresses.

1) N: flat lacking   2) ♭ in both MSS
    V: ♯ (by mistake?)
3) Bass bars 136-149 in tenor clef in both N and V, although V mistakenly continues F clef.
4) c″ instead of d″ in both MSS.

1) Copied up a 3rd (surely by mistake!) in both MSS.

1) When Nerone is sung by a tenor, the d', c♯', and d' must also be transposed down an octave.

N: Subito ch'há detto à Dio Poppea ben mio si fá il seguente Ritornello et poi segue scena 4ª
As soon as he has said 'Farewell Poppaea, I leave you', the ensuing Ritornello is performed, and then scene 4.

A comparison of Monteverdi's *Orfeo,* written for the court of Mantua in 1607, and his *L'incoronazione di Poppea* ("The Coronation of Poppea"), written for the Teatro Grimano in Venice in the season of 1642–1643, illustrates the differences between courtly opera of the early 17th century and public opera of the mid-17th century. *Orfeo,* for all its stylistic variety, is serious from beginning to end, without an ounce of comic relief. *Poppea,* in contrast, mixes high seriousness with comic scenes. It also requires relatively little in the way of chorus and orchestra and has no scenes that call for elaborate sets or machinery. *Poppea*'s very human characters, drawn from history, contrast vividly with the mythic, allegorical characters in *Orfeo.* Nero, the Emperor of Rome, is married to Ottavia but hopelessly in love with Poppea, who in turn is married to Ottone. Smitten by his love for Poppea, Nero turns to putty in her hands. At Poppea's urging, he banishes her husband to exile, divorces his own wife, and puts to death the philosopher Seneca for the simple reason that his moralizing is inconvenient for her. Poppea is, in short, a close cousin to Lady Macbeth, a very realistic personality whose lust for power leads her to cut down everything in her path.

This is scarcely the kind of scenario one finds in courtly opera, in which the heroes and heroines are unfailingly strong and virtuous. But it is precisely the type of story that would have appealed to a broader, less aristocratic audience. Monteverdi was not writing for the lower classes, to be sure—that portion of the public could not afford tickets to the opera and probably would not have attended in any event—but he was writing for the lesser nobility, businessmen, bankers, and the huge influx of visiting dignitaries that came to Venice for Carnival season every year. Opera soon became a big business in its own right.

As in *Orfeo,* Monteverdi uses a variety of dramatic and musical strategies to create a story that is consistently fast-paced. The prologue to *Poppea* opens with a quarrel between Fortune (Fate) and Virtue, each of whom claims to be the more powerful. Love, a child-like cupid figure, intervenes to remind them that in spite of his small stature, he is in fact far more powerful than either Fate or Virtue, and he shows them the story of Poppea to prove his point.

As the curtain rises on Act I, Ottone arrives home late one night to find Nero's bodyguards at his door. Ottone's opening number (Scene 1) flows seamlessly into a comic dialogue between the two guards; at the beginning of Scene 2, in fact, we hear the closing lines of Ottone's despair as he hides himself in the shadows. We then hear the extended dialogue (Scene 3) between Nero and Poppea. The juxtaposition of serious and humorous, lyrical and declamatory is readily apparent in this sequence. The boundary between recitative and aria, which would become more pronounced in the opera of the later 17th and 18th centuries, is still quite fluid here.

79 Heinrich Schütz (1585–1672): Singet dem Herren ein neues Lied, SWV 342 (1647)

((•●Listen
CD4   Track 13
mysearchlab (with scrolling translation)
Book p. 223

Singet dem Herren ein neues Lied,
singet dem Herren alle Welt.
Singet dem Herrn und lobet seinen Namen.
Prediget einen Tag am andern sein Heil.
Erzählet unter den Heiden seine Ehre,
unter allen Völkern seine Wunder.
Denn der Herr ist groß und hoch zu loben,
wunderbarlich über alle Götter.

O sing unto the Lord a new song:
sing unto the Lord all the earth.
Sing unto the Lord, bless his name;
shew forth his salvation from day to day.
Declare his glory among the heathen,
his wonders among all people.
For the Lord is great, and greatly to be praised:
For he is to be feared above all gods.

Psalm 96: 1–4

80 Schütz: Motet
Saul, was verfolgst du mich?
SWV 415 (1650)

((•◦—Listen
CD4 Track 14
mysearchlab
Book p. 223

Composers applied the principles of the *seconda prattica* to sacred as well as secular music. Heinrich Schütz's *Singet dem Herren ein neues Lied* ("Sing Unto the Lord a New Song") owes much to the "new practice." Schütz may or may not have actually studied with Monteverdi in Venice, but he was certainly aware of the older composer's music.

The two solo violin lines of this work operate at times in counterpoint to the tenor solo, at times as an antiphonal "choir" of their own. Every verse or half-verse of the psalm text (Psalm 96: 1–4) is differentiated by a new musical idea, yet the individual sections are connected through a slow but steady increase in register, rhythmic motion, and melodic intensity. In a series of carefully graduated steps, the listener is moved from stasis to a state of spiritual ecstasy at the end.

Herausgeber: Günter Graulich
Generalbaßaussetzung: Paul Horn
English text by Derek McCulloch

194

No. 80 Schütz: Saul, was verfolgst du mich?   ■ **195**

Like Monteverdi, Schütz never abandoned the *prima prattica* entirely. On the contrary, he believed that training in *prima prattica* counterpoint was essential for aspiring composers. Still, even in a polychoral motet like *Saul, was verfolgst du mich?* he incorporates distinct traits of the *seconda prattica*. In a moment of high drama, Saul (later to become the Apostle Paul) is struck blind on the road to Damascus and hears the voice of the resurrected Christ calling to him: "Saul, Saul, why dost thou persecute me?" The opening cry rises out of the low depths of the bass, punctuated by the basso continuo, eventually swelling into the combined voices of two four-part choirs, six soloists, and two additional lines for unspecified treble instruments (usually played by violins). The echo of the cry is not just softer but eerily different in timbre (m. 21–23). God's words to Saul continue with a series of lines distributed among the various vocal and instrumental forces. Solo passages alternate with choral and instrumental sections. The words rush ahead at times, hold back at others; certain of them (such as *löcken,* "to kick") are emphasized through the use of melisma, while others ("Saul") make their effect through simpler declamation. The cumulative effect is stunning as it captures the reverberations of God's words in Saul's mind at the very moment in which Saul is struck blind.

Performance notes: Schütz calls in the score for two violins "or their equivalent." In this recording, these parts are performed on the cornetto, a Renaissance forerunner of the trumpet. The continuo consists of organ, theorbo (a large lute with an extended neck), and violone (literally, a "large violin"), a forerunner of today's double bass.

81 Jean-Baptiste Lully (1632–1687): Opera **Armide,** Overture and Act II, Scene 5 (1686)

* See Introduction regarding instrumentation.

Scène 5

Renaud endormy, Armide

177

'Armide tenant un dard à la main'

'Armide va pour fraper Renaud, et ne peut executer le dessein qu'elle a de luy oster la vie.'

'Les Demons transformez en Zephirs, enlevent Renaud et Armide.'

ARMIDE	ARMIDE
(tenant un dard à la main)	(holding a spear in her hand)
Enfin il est en ma puissance,	Finally he is in my power,
Ce fatal ennemi, ce superbe vainqueur.	this fatal enemy, this superb warrior.
Le charme du sommeil le livre à ma vengeance;	The charm of sleep delivers him to my vengeance;
Je vais percer son invincible coeur.	I will pierce his invincible heart.
Par lui tous mes captifs sont sortis d'esclavage;	Through him all my captives have escaped from slavery.
Qu'il éprouve toute ma rage.	Let him feel all my anger.
Quel trouble me saisit? qui me fait hésiter?	What fear grips me? what makes me hesitate?
(Armide va pour frapper Renaud	(Armide moves to strike Rinaldo
et ne peut executer le dessein	but cannot carry out her plan
qu'elle a de luy oster la vie)	to take his life)
Qu'est-ce qu'en sa faveur la pitié me veut dire?	What in his favor does pity want to tell me?
Frappons … Ciel! qui peut m'arrêter?	Let us strike … Heavens! Who can stop me?
Achevons … je frémis! vengeons-nous … je soupire!	Let us get on with it … I tremble! Let us avenge … I sigh!
Est-ce ainsi que je dois me venger aujourd'hui?	Is it thus that I must avenge myself today?
Ma colère s'éteint quand j'approche de lui.	My rage is extinguished when I approach him.
Plus je le vois, plus ma vengeance est vaine;	The more I see of him, the more my vengeance is ineffectual.
Mon bras tremblant se refuse à ma haine.	My trembling arm denies my hate.
Ah! quelle cruauté de lui ravir le jour!	Ah! What cruelty, to rob him of the light of day!
A ce jeune héros tout cède sur la terre.	To this young hero everything on earth surrenders.
Qui croirait qu'il fut né seulement pour la guerre?	Who would believe that he was born only for war?
Il semble être fait pour l'Amour.	He seems to be made for love.
Ne puis-je me venger à moins qu'il ne périsse?	Could I not avenge myself unless he dies?
Hé! ne suffit-il pas que l'amour le punisse?	Oh, is it not enough that Love should punish him?
Puisqu'il n'a pu trouver mes yeux assez charmants,	Since he could not find my eyes charming enough,
Qu'il m'aime au moins par mes enchantements.	let him love me at least through my sorcery,
Que, s'il se peut, je le haïsse.	so that, if it's possible, I may hate him.
Venez, venez, seconder mes désirs,	Come, come support my desires,
Démons, transformez-vous en d'aimables zéphirs.	demons; transform yourselves into friendly zephyrs.
Je cède à ce vainqueur, la pitié me surmonte.	I give in to this conqueror; pity overwhelms me.
Cachez ma foiblesse et ma honte	Conceal my weakness and my shame
Dans les plus reculés déserts.	in the most remote desert.
Volez, volez, conduisez-nous au bout de l'univers.	Fly, fly, lead us to the end of the universe.
(Les demons transformez en	(The demons are transformed in
Zephirs, enlevent Renaud et Armide)	zephyrs, lifting up Rinaldo and Armida)

—Philippe Quinault

Lully and his librettist Philippe Quinault (1635–1688) drew on classical mythology and chivalric romances for subject matter for their operas, but the plots were widely understood as veiled commentaries (always favorable, of course) on recent events at court. The hero of any given opera was almost invariably understood to be an allegorical counterpart to Louis XIV. In *Armide,* the hero Renaud obeys the call of duty and spurns the enchantment of the sorceress for whom the opera is named.

The overture to *Armide* moves from a slow introduction with dotted rhythms to a fast imitative section. The dotted rhythms, associated with royalty, were an homage to the splendor of the king. This form eventually came to be known as the French overture and would be adopted by many composers—Italian and German as well as French—over subsequent decades.

In the widely admired scene toward the end of Act II of *Armide,* the sorceress Armida is about to kill the crusader-knight Renaud (Rinaldo), who is asleep under her spell. But she cannot bring herself to do the deed: she hates Renaud because he is indifferent to her beauty, yet she also loves him. The opera, based on Torquato Tasso's epic poem *Gerusalemme liberata* ("Jerusalem Liberated"), will end badly for Armida—Rinaldo's love for her, induced through spells, does not last—but for the moment, she is in complete command of everything but herself. The scene divides into two sections: (1) Armida's monologue and (2) a summons to her assisting demons. The opening monologue moves fluidly through a large quantity of text. The declamation here is more melodic than most Italian recitative. The opening thematic idea will in fact provide the basis for the more dance-like second part of this scene.

Performance notes: The notated rhythms are not observed strictly. This is in keeping with all that we know about performance practice in France during the Baroque era. Dotted values are exaggerated, with the longer notes made longer and the shorter ones shorter; dotted eighth notes followed by a sixteenth, for example, are performed like double-dotted eighths followed by a thirty-second note, as at the very beginning of the overture. This practice is known as *overdotting*. And runs notated in rhythms of equal value are not always performed in uniform rhythm; instead, some are lengthened while others are shortened to compensate. The eighth notes in the bass line throughout the overture's slow introduction, for example, are played in unequal time values. This practice, known by its French designation of *notes inégales* ("unequal notes"), is left to the discretion of the orchestra's leader. The sound of wind at the beginning of Act II, Scene 5, comes from a machine built specially for this purpose. Opera producers took great pride in special effects of all kind, including sound effects.

82 George Frideric Handel (1685–1759): Opera **Giulio Cesare,** Act I, Scenes 5–7 (1724)

CD5   Tracks 1–3
mysearchlab (with scrolling translation)
Book p. 231

205

SCENA VII.

Quartieri nel campo di CESARE con l'urna nel mezzo, ove
sono le ceneri del capo di POMPEO, sopra eminente cumulo di trofei.

CESARE, poi CURIO, che introduce CLEOPATRA e NIRENO.

SCENA V

CLEOPATRA
Regni Cleopatra; ed al mio seggio intorno
popolo adorator arabo e siro
su questo crin la sacra benda adori:

sù, chi di voi, miei fidi,
ha petto e cor di sollevarmi al trono,

giuri su questa destra eterna fede.

NIRENO
Reina, infausti eventi!

CLEOPATRA
Che fia? ché tardi?

NIRENO
Troncar fé Tolomeo
il capo …

CLEOPATRA
Ohimè, di chi?

NIRENO
Del gran Pompeo.

CLEOPATRA
Stelle! Costui che apporta?

NIRENO
Per stabilirsi al soglio
a Cesare mandò fra doni involto …

CLEOPATRA
Che gli mandò?

NIRENO
L'esanimato volto.

CLEOPATRA
Sù, partite miei fidi; e tu qui resta.

Alle cesaree tende
son risolta portarmi,
e tu, Nireno, mi servirai di scorta.

NIRENO
Che dirà Tolomeo?

SCENE 5

CLEOPATRA
Let Cleopatra reign, and around my throne
Let the adoring peoples of Arabia and Syria
Prostrate themselves before the sacred band
   that engirds my tresses.
Come, let those of you
Who have the mind and heart to raise me upon
   the throne
Swear eternal loyalty on my right hand.

NIRENUS
O Queen, ill-starred events!

CLEOPATRA
What has happened? Why do you delay?

NIRENUS
Ptolemy has
beheaded …

CLEOPATRA
O heavens! Whom?

NIRENUS
The great Pompey.

CLEOPATRA
Gods in heaven! What news does this man
   bring?

NIRENUS
To ascertain his throne he sent it,
Among other gifts, wrapped in a veil, to
   Caesar …

CLEOPATRA
What did he send?

NIRENUS
The lifeless head.

CLEOPATRA
Go, withdraw, my loyal subjects. You remain
   here.
I have resolved to betake
Myself to Caesar's camp,
And you, Nirenus, shall serve as my escort.

NIRENUS
What will Ptolomy say?

CLEOPATRA
Non paventar: col guardo,
meglio ch'egli non fece
col capo di Pompeo,
Cesare obligherò.
Invano aspira al trono:
egli è il germano, e la regina io sono.

TOLOMEO
Tu di regnar pretendi,
donna superba e altera?

CLEOPATRA
Io ciò ch'è mio contendo; e la corona
dovuta alla mia fronte
giustamente pretendo.

TOLOMEO
Vanne, e torna omai, folle,
a qual di donna è l'uso:
di scettro invece, a trattar l'ago e il fuso.

CLEOPATRA
Anzi, tu pur, effeminato amante,
va' dell'età sui primi nati albori,
di regno invece, a coltivar gli amori!

  Non disperar, chi sa?
se al regno non l'avrai,
avrai sorte in amor.
  Mirando una beltà
in essa troverai
a consolar un cor.

SCENA VI

ACHILLA
Sire, signor!

TOLOMEO
  Achilla!
Come fu il capo tronco
da Cesare gradito?

ACHILLA
Sdegnò l'opra.

TOLOMEO
  Che sento?

CLEOPATRA
Have no fear. With a single look alone
I shall be able to compel Caesar
Better than he did
With the head of Pompey.
In vain he aspires to the throne:
He is my brother, and I am the queen.

PTOLOMY (enters)
You pretend to the throne,
Proud and presumptuous woman?

CLEOPATRA
I contest what is mine, and rightfully
Claim the crown
That belongs to my brow.

PTOLOMY
Get you gone and return, you madwoman,
To your proper place as a woman:
Wield the needle and the distaff instead of the
  sceptre.

CLEOPATRA
It is rather you, effeminate lover,
You, who are still in the dawn of your life,
To go and cultivate your loves instead of the
  kingdom!
  Do not despair: who knows,
But that you will have the luck in reigning
That you have in love.
  Gazing on your beauty
You find in it the way
To beguile a heart.
                    (Exits)

SCENE 6

ACHILLA
Sire! Lord!

PTOLOMY
  Achilla!
How did the severed head
Of Pompey please Caesar?

ACHILLA
He despised the deed.

PTOLOMY
  What do I hear?

ACHILLA
T'accusò d'inesperto e troppo ardito.

TOLOMEO
Tant' osa un vil romano?

ACHILLA
  Il mio consiglio
apprendi, o Tolomeo:
verrà Cesare in corte; in tua vendetta
cada costui, come cadé Pompeo.

TOLOMEO
Chi condurrà l'impresa?

ACHILLA
  Io ti prometto
darti estinto il superbo al regio piede,
se di Pompeo la moglie
in premio a me il tuo voler concede.

TOLOMEO
È costei tanto vaga?

ACHILLA
Lega col crine, e col bel volto impiaga.

TOLOMEO
Amico, il tuo consiglio è la mia stella.
Vanne, pensa e poi torna.

Muora Cesare, muora; e il capo altero

sia del mio piè sostegno.
Roma, oppressa da lui, libera vada,
e fermezza al mio regno
sia la morte di lui più che la spada.
  L'empio, sleale, indegno
vorria rapirmi il regno,
e disturbar così
la pace mia.
  Ma perda pur la vita,
prima che in me tradita
dall'avido suo cor
la fede sia.

ACHILLA
He accused you of misconduct and impudence.

PTOLOMY
A vile Roman has the effrontery?

ACHILLA
  Listen
To my advice, Ptolomy!
Caesar is coming to the court; let him fall victim
To your revenge as Pompey fell.

PTOLOMY
Who will undertake the business?

ACHILLA
  I promise
To lay the haughty corpse at your royal feet,
If in recompense you are willing
To grant me Pompey's wife.

PTOLOMY
Is she so desirable?

ACHILLA
She captivates one with her tresses and pierces
  one's heart with her fair face.

PTOLOMY
Friend, your counsel will be my guiding star:
Go, reflect and return.

Let Caesar die! Let him die! And his proud
  head
Sustain my footing. Let Rome,
Whom he oppresses, regain her freedom,
And his death, more than my sword,
Ascertain my rule.
  The infidel, traitor, villain
  Would rob me of my throne
  And thereby trouble
  My peace of mind.
  But rather let him lose his life
  Before my confidence
  Be betrayed
  By his avaricious heart!

SCENA VII	SCENE 7
CESARE	CAESAR

Alma del gran Pompeo,
che al cener suo d'intorno
invisibil t'aggiri,
fur ombra i tuoi trofei,
ombra la tua grandezza, e un'ombra sei.

Così termina alfine il fasto umano.
Ieri chi vivo occupò un mondo in guerra,
oggi risolto in polve un'urna serra.

Tal di ciascuno, ahi lasso,
il principio è di terra e il fine è un sasso.
Misera vita, oh quanto è fral tuo stato!
Ti forma un soffio, e ti distrugge un fiato.

Soul of great Pompey
That hovers invisible
About your ashes,
Your victories were but a shadow,
A shadow was your greatness, and you yourself
are but a shadow.
To this end comes man's glory.
Yesterday he, who alive, engaged a world in war,
Is today dissolved into ash and is enclosed in an
urn.
Such, alas, is the fate of everyone,
The beginning is earth, the end a stone.
Wretched life! O, how frail is your condition!
A sigh forms you, a breath destroys you.

Ptolomy (Tolomeo), co-ruler of Egypt with his sister, Cleopatra, is threatened by the arrival of the conquering Julius Ceaesar (Giulio Cesare). To appease Caesar, Ptolomy presents him with the severed head of Caesar's Roman rival, Pompey. But Caesar is disgusted by such barbarism and rejects the gift. In the *recitativo semplice*—"simple recitative," accompanied only by the basso continuo—that opens Act I, Scene 5, Cleopatra learns of these events from Nirenus (Nireno); her brother Ptolomy then enters the scene, and they exchange rapid-fire barbs.

One of the structural conventions of opera seria is an underlying alternation of recitative and aria. Cleopatra's aria (*Non disperar*) sets itself off from the preceding recitative not only through its melody and orchestration, but also through its text: arias are typically written as poetic verse, not prose. Like so many arias in opera seria, this is a da capo aria, with the opening A section repeated (and embellished) after the conclusion of the contrasting B section.

Ptolomy, having discussed (in recitative) his plans with his aide Achilla, launches into his own da capo aria in Scene 6 (*L'empio, sleale, indegno*). This aria begins with an orchestral ritornello (Ritornello 1) that at once establishes the key, mood, and theme of the aria as a whole. The opening solo (Solo 1) reiterates the orchestral material in the same key, but now with words. The voice eventually carries the music from E♭ major to B♭ major (m. 32), and the new key signals the onset of Ritornello 2. This brief return of the instruments alone offers the singer the opportunity to catch his breath. The soloist reenters in m. 36 and guides the music through a variety of keys before finally bringing it to the dominant at m. 58. This half cadence is a signal to orchestra and audience alike that the cadenza is about to begin. From the Italian word for "cadence," the cadenza is a truly soloistic moment, with no accompaniment of the orchestra at all; the soloist instead improvises (or at least gives the appearance of improvising), invariably with great virtuosity. Cadenzas are typically indicated in the score of an aria by a simple fermata sign, and the cadenza in the da capo performance of the A section was expected to be even more flamboyant than in the first. After this display of unaccompanied virtuosity, the second solo section concludes on the tonic (m. 61). At this point the third and final ritornello enters to bring this section of the aria—and on its return *da capo*, the entire aria—to closure in the tonic.

HANDEL, *GIULIO CESARE*, ACT I, *L'EMPIO, SLEALE, INDEGNO*: THE A SECTION.						
	Rit. 1	Solo 1	Rit. 2	Solo 2	Cadenza	Cadenza Rit. 3
Measure	1	12	32	36	58	61
Key	E♭ major	E♭ major	B♭ major	Unstable	V/E♭ major	E♭ major
Harmony	I		V		V/I	I

The ritornello principle is reinforced by the tonal structure: the A section begins and ends in the tonic, with a contrasting key in between. The B section, in C minor, beginning at the words *Mà perda pur la vita* is even briefer and consists of a single solo unit; there is no ritornello within this section. When considered within the context of the aria as a whole, however, this B section is framed by two ritornello passages: Ritornello 3 from the end of A, and Ritornello 1 from the da capo resumption of the aria's beginning. In a sense, then, the B section as a whole can be seen as a large Solo 3.

HANDEL, *GIULIO CESARE*, ACT I, *L'EMPIO, SLEALE, INDEGNO*: THE STRUCTURE OF THE WHOLE IN PERFORMANCE.										
A					B	A (da capo)				
Rit. 1	Solo 1	Rit. 2	Solo 2	Rit. 3	Solo 3	Rit. 4	Solo 4	Rit. 5	Solo 5	Rit. 6
I		V		I	vi	I		V		I

The next scene is one of quiet contemplation. Julius Caesar is at the tomb of the murdered Pompey and reflects on the brevity of human life. Here, Handel uses *recitativo accompagnato*, that is, accompanied recitative, supported or punctuated by the full orchestra rather than the basso continuo alone. This type of recitative was used sparingly in opera seria and ususally reserved for moments of high emotion and drama.

Performance notes: In keeping with performance practices of Handel's time, both soloists in this recording embroider the A section of their respective arias with considerable embellishments. The soprano Barbara Schlick (Cleopatra) uses rapid figuration to display the agility of her voice and transposes the whole note B in m. 20 up an entire octave to display her impressive range. She goes on to interpolate a miniature cadenza at m. 35, slowing down the tempo for dramatic effect. The countertenor Derek Lee Ragin (Ptolomy) adds similar embellishments to the written score, even during the intitial performance of the aria's A section. The high outbursts show his voice to good advantange and are at the same time in keeping with the mood of outrage expressed by his character.

83 Henry Purcell (1659–1695):
Opera **Dido and Aeneas**, Act I
(excerpt) (1689)

((•◦ **Listen**

CD5 Tracks 4–9
mysearchlab
Book p. 241

ACT I.

Scene. *The Palace. Enter Dido, Belinda, and train.*

Nº 1. SCENA and CHORUS.

Note: The harpsichord part here is the editor's realization of the basso continuo part.

The origins and early performance history of Purcell's opera *Dido and Aeneas* remain shrouded in mystery. We know it was first performed by the students at a school for young ladies in Chelsea (west of London at the time), but the next known performance, in a drastically altered version, did not occur until 1700, and the earliest surviving musical sources date from well after the composer's death. *Dido and Aeneas* may have been suppressed for political reasons, either by Purcell himself or by the authorities, on the grounds of its potentially unflattering commentary on the dual reign of King William, a foreigner, and Queen Mary, daughter of Charles I. The plot, after all, deals with a foreign prince who promises to marry the Queen of Carthage, then reneges and abandons her, driving her to suicide.

The foreign prince is Aeneas, a refugee from fallen Troy, who is on his way to Italy with his companions to found the city of Rome in fulfillment of a promise from the gods. They land in Carthage, ruled by Queen Dido. Aeneas and Dido are smitten with one another. She, with great foreboding, knowing his destiny, lets herself be wooed. He pledges to abandon his promised Rome. But when a witch disguised as Mercury, the messenger of the gods, orders him to leave, he obeys and abandons Dido. She, disconsolate, dies, but not before singing an exquisite lament.

Purcell's opera owes much to the French tradition, beginning with the overture, a slow introduction followed by an imitative fast section. The singing moves rapidly and fluently, with a minimum of virtuosity and no *da capo* arias. Act I opens with a rapid sequence of brief numbers. Belinda, Dido's confidante, urges her mistress to shake off her grief, and the chorus echoes her thoughts in a kind of communal commentary. Dido makes her entrance with a lament over a ground bass, prefiguring her celebrated (but dramatically more static) lament at the very end of the opera. This brief number gives way to an exchange in simple recitative, in which Belinda forces Dido to confront her love of Aeneas. This exchange segues into a song extolling the virtues of a union between Carthage and Troy ("The greatest blessing…") which moves to a chorus ("When monarchs unite"). The recitative dialogue between Dido and Belinda resumes, leading in turn to a duet ("Fear no danger to ensue") and chorus.

Performance notes: This recording uses a variety of different instrumental combinations for the basso continuo: combinations of harpsichord, theorbo (a long-necked lute), bass violin (slightly larger than the modern-day cello), and, in the Duet and Chorus No. 6 ("Fear no danger to ensue"), guitars, a very popular instrument in Purcell's time. Thus, whereas the modern-day edition indicates simply "harpsichord," an imaginative performance like this one can invest the work with far more timbral variety.

John Gay (1685–1732) and
Johann Christoph Pepusch
(1667–1752): **The Beggar's Opera**
(excerpts) (1728)

(((•• **Listen**
CD5   Tracks 10–12
mysearchlab
Book p. 241

AIR I. An old woman clothed in gray.

AIR VII. Oh *London* is a fine town.

AIR VIII. Grim King of the ghosts, &c.

Can Love be con-troul'd by ad-vice? Will Cu-pid our Moth-ers o-

bey? Though my heart were as fro-zen as Ice. At his flame 'twould have melt-ed a-

way. When he kist me so close-ly he prest. Twas so sweet that I must have com-

ply'd. So I thought it both saf-est and best To mar-ry, for fear you should chide.

In 1728, the playwright John Gay achieved a rousing success with *The Beggar's Opera,* an English-language semi-opera that portrayed common criminals rather than mythological figures or historical heroes. Gay set his words to existing tunes and engaged the German-born Johann Christoph Pepusch (1667–1752) to provide the accompaniments. The arrangements are quite simple, and the dialogue is spoken rather than sung. As the Beggar explains at the outset: "I hope I may be forgiven, that I have not made my Opera throughout unnatural, like those in vogue; for I have no Recitative."

The original libretto of this ballad opera features 69 songs, of which 28 have been identified as English ballads, while another 23 derive from popular songs of Irish, Scottish, or French origin. *The Beggar's Opera* is full of political references that delighted contemporary audiences. Whereas the French overture was always understood to be in honor of the King, the overture to *The Beggar's Opera* quotes the song *Walpole, or the Happy Clown,* a ditty attacking Robert Walpole, prime minister of Great Britain at the time. *The Beggar's Opera* was an enormous commercial success and was soon being performed as far away as Charleston, South Carolina, and Williamsburg, Virginia; it is said to have been George Washington's favorite opera. It continued to be performed in one version or another at least once a year for the rest of the 18th century. The work took on new life in a German adaptation by Bertholt Brecht in 1928 entitled *Die Dreigroschenoper*—"The Threepenny Opera"—with music by Kurt Weill.

---

85 Giacomo Carissimi (1605–1674): ((•──Listen
Jephte (excerpt) (ca. 1645–1649)
CD5 Track 13
mysearchlab (with scrolling translation)
Book p. 245

Revised and edited by
Janet Beat

HISTORICUS
ALTO

Cum vo-cas-set in proe-li-um fi-li-os Is-ra-el rex fi-li-

ORGAN

o-rum Am-mon, et ver-bis Jeph-te ac-qui-es-ce-re no-lu-is-set,

fac-tus est su-per Jeph-te Spi-ri-tus Do-mi-ni, et pro-

1) Bar 23, Soprano III. ♩. ♪ in A
2) Bar 27, Bass. ♫ ♪ in A

3) Bar 35, Continuo in A reads 𝄢 but Charpentier has written beneath it the version here given with the legend 'Caris.' (? Carissimi).

4) Bar 37, Continuo in A reads 𝄢 but again Charpentier has written beneath it the version here given with the same legend.

8) Bar 62, Soprano III. ♩♪ in A

* Bars 70-71. There is much to be said for taking this organ bass an octave higher.

HISTORICUS
SOPRANO

Et per-cus-sit Jeph-te vi-gin-ti ci-vi-ta-tes Am-mon pla-ga mag-na, pla-ga mag-na ni - mis.

78   76   76 5 4 3

3:49   **TRIO** *(a few voices only)*

SI
Et u-lu-lan-tes fi-li-i Am-mon,

SII
Et u-lu-lan-tes fi-li-i Am - mon, fac-ti

A
Et u-lu-lan-tes fi-li-i Am - mon, fac-ti

♩=66

78 ♭   6   6   6 4 #3 ♭

fac - ti sunt co-ram fi-li-is Is-ra-el hu - mi-li-a - ti.

sunt co-ram fi-li-is Is - ra-el hu-mi-li-a - ti.

sunt co-ram fi-li-is Is - ra - el hu - mi-li-a - ti.

88 6   6#   6 4 5 3   6 5   5 4 3

*Bars 78-88. There is much to be said for taking this organ bass an octave higher.

HISTORICUS

Cum vocasset in proelium filios Israel rex filiorum Ammon, et verbis Jephte acquiescere noluisset, factus est super Jephte Spiritus Domini, et progressus ad filios Ammon votum vovit Domini dicens:

JEPHTE

Si tradiderit Dominus filios Ammon in manus meas, quicumque primus de domo mea occurrerit mihi, offeram illum Domino in holocaustum.

CHORUS

Transivit ergo Jephte ad filios Ammon, ut in spiritu forti et virtute Domini pugnaret contra eos.

DUET

Et clangebant tubae, et personabant tympana, et proelium commissum est adversus Ammon.

BASS SOLO

Fugite, cedite, impii, perite gentes, occumbite in gladio; Dominus exercituum in proelium surrexit, et pugnat contra vos.

CHORUS

Fugite, cedite, impii, corruite, et in furore gladii dissipamini.

HISTORICUS

Et percussit Jephte viginti civitates Ammon plaga magna nimis.

TRIO

Et ululantes filii Ammon, facti sunt coram filiis Israel humiliati.

When the king of the children of Ammon made war against the children of Israel, and hearkened not unto the words of Jephthah, then there came upon Jephthah the Spirit of the Lord, and he went up against the children of Ammon and vowed unto the Lord, saying:

If thou shalt indeed deliver the children of Ammon into my hands, whatsoever first cometh forth of the doors of my house to meet me, I will offer to the Lord for a burnt offering.

Then Jephthah passed over to the children of Ammon, and he fought in the spirit and the strength of God against them.

And the trumpets sounded, and the drums were beaten, when battle was joined against the children of Ammon.

Flee from us, yield to us, impious ones, give away, ye heathen, and fall before our mighty sword; for the God of Israel is risen up to battle and fights against our foes.

Flee from us, yield to us, impious ones, we scatter you, and with our keen and glittering swords we hew you down.

Jephthah therefore smote them, and took from them twenty cities, and there was a grievous slaughter.

And he subdued the children of Ammon, for the Lord delivered them to the children of Israel.

Giacomo Carissimi's *Jephte* was one of the most popular of all early oratorios. The Latin-language libretto, based on the book of Judges 11, tells the story of Jephte (also spelled Jephthah), an Israelite general who promises to sacrifice to God the first thing to emerge from his house on his homecoming if God grants him victory in an impending battle. Returning home victorious, Jephte is dismayed to see his only daughter emerge first from his house to greet him. She, virtuously, urges him to fulfill his vow. The work ends with an extended lament by the daughter (who has no name, either in the Bible or in this oratorio) and her companions. In Carissimi's setting, a narrator designated as the Historicus—at times a bass, at times an alto—introduces the characters and keeps the plot moving forward in brisk fashion. Except for this narrative device and the fact that it is sung in Latin, *Jephthe* is musically indistinguishable from operas of the mid-17th century. Like them it places a premium on vocal virtuosity and features a quick succession of short movements, some for solo, some for a small group of soloists, others still for chorus.

Performance notes: The ensemble in this recording performs the duet *Et clangebant* (track 38) as a duet of soprano recorders before presenting it vocally. Although marked "organ" in this edition, the continuo part can in fact be interpreted by any chordal instrument. This recording uses at various times theorbo and harpsichord as well as organ.

86   Handel: Anthem
Zadok the Priest (1727)

((•─ **Listen**
CD5   Track 14
mysearchlab
Book p. 248

Note: The pianoforte part in this score is for rehearsal purposes only and is not part of Handel's original score.

Elisabeth Jacquet de la Guerre (1665–1729): **"Le coup est achevé"** from **Judith** (1708)

((•—Listen

CD5   Track 15
mysearchlab (with scrolling translation)
Book p. 248

Many religious anthems were tailored to fit quite practical needs. The long orchestral introduction to Handel's *Zadok the Priest*, for example, allowed the royal procession sufficient time to make its way down the long center aisle of Westminster Abbey for the coronation of King George II in 1727. The effect of the swelling orchestra, the dramatic entrance of the voices, and the arrival of the new king were of such overwhelming effect that the anthem has been used in every British coronation since that time. The emphasis on chordal declamation reinforces the sense of unity within the chorus and, by extension, with the nation as a whole.

Air.	Air.
Le coup est achevé,	The blow is struck,
Quelle gloire éclatante,	What a glorious victory:
Judith est triomphante,	Judith is triumphant,
Israël est sauvé!	Israel is saved!
Pour ce Guerrier trop tendre,	For this too tender warrior,
Il n'est plus de reveil,	There is no more awakening,
La mort vient de le prendre	Death has just taken him
Dans les bras du sommeil.	In the arms of sleep.

Throughout the Baroque era the term *cantata* denoted both small- and large-scale works, ranging from a solo singer with basso continuo to a large ensemble of chorus, soloists, and instruments. A cantata could be a single movement or multiple movements.

Many 17th-century cantatas are works in the tradition of the solo madrigal. This includes the cantatas of Elisabeth Jacquet de la Guerre, which she published in three sets. "Le coup est achevé" is an air from *Judith* (1708), based on the Apochryphal book in which a Jewish woman saves the town of Bethulia (near Jerusalem). She enters the camp of Holofernes, commander-in-chief of the armies of Nebuchadnezzar, with a promise of information to help him seize the town. He gets drunk and falls asleep, and Judith, with the help of her maid, decapitates him and uses the head to frighten and disperse the assailants of Bethulia.

The cantata is performed by one singer, basso continuo, and an obbligato violin. The singer is a sympathetic narrator who exhorts Judith to accomplish her task, and alternately plays the role of the would-be seducer and mocks him. In an arioso, she expresses Judith's emotions as she prepares to "strike the blow"—after which she sings the celebratory air ("Le coup est achevé") and a hymn of thanks to "the only ruler of kings." The overall key is A major, with excursions to A minor and E minor.

88 Johann Sebastian Bach (1685–1750): Cantata **Jesu, der du meine Seele,** BWV 78 (excerpts) (1724)

((•—Listen
CD5 Tracks 16–20
mysearchlab (with scrolling translation)
Book p. 249

2. Aria. Duetto

1. Chorus: Jesu, der du meine Seele

Jesu, der du meine Seele hast durch deinen
  bittern Tod

aus des Teufels finstrer Höhle und der schweren
  Seelennoth

kräftiglich herausgerissen,

und mich Solches lassen wissen

durch dein angenehmes Wort:

sei doch jetzt, o Gott, mein Hort!

Jesus, thou who my soul has, through your
  bitter death,

from the devil's dark hell and the severe
  need of the soul

powerfully lifted out,

and gave this known to me

through your comforting word:

Be thou now, o God, my protection!

2. Aria (Duet): Wir eilen

Wir eilen mit schwachen, doch emsigen Schritten,
o Jesu, o Meister, zu helfen zu dir.
Du suchest die Kranken und Irrenden treulich.
Ach! höre, wie wir die Stimme erheben,
um Hülfe zu bitten!
Es sei uns dein gnädiges Antlitz erfreulich!

We hasten with weak, yet eager steps,
oh Jesus, oh Master, for help toward thee.
You visit the sick and wayward faithfully.
Ah! hear, how we our voices lift
for help to ask
May us your graceful countenance brighten!

3. and 4. Recitative and Aria (omitted here)

5. Recitative: Die Wunden

Die Wunden, Nägel, Kron' und Grab,
die Schläge, so man dort dem Heiland gab,
sind ihm nunmehro Siegeszeichen,
und können mir erneute Kräfte reichen.
Wenn ein erschreckliches Gericht
den Fluch für die Verdammten spricht:
so kehrst du ihm in Segen.
Mich kann kein Schmerz und keine Pein
  bewegen,
weil sie mein Heiland kennt,
und da dein Herz für mich in Liebe brennt,
so lege ich hinwieder das meine vor dir nieder.
Dies, mein Herz, mit Leid vermenget,
so dein theures Blut besprenget,
so am Kreuz vergossen ist,
geb' ich dir, Herr Jesu Christ.

The wounds, nails, crown, and grave,
the blows, that were given the Saviour there
are to him now signs of victory
and can to me renewed powers give.
If a terrible court
the curse of the damned pronounces:
so shall you reverse it [the curse] into a blessing.
No suffering and no pain can move me.

Because my Saviour knows them [too],
and because your heart for me in love burns,
thus I present back to you my heart.
This, my heart, with suffering heaped,
as your dear blood flows,
as it on the cross poured out,
so give I myself to you, Lord Jesus Christ.

6. Aria: Nun du wirst mein Gewissen stillen

Nun du wirst mein Gewissen stillen,
So wider mich um Rache schreit,

Ja, deine Treue wird's erfüllen,
Weil mir dein Wort die Hoffnung beut.
Wenn Christen an dich glauben,
Wird sie kein Feind in Ewigkeit
Aus deinen Händen rauben.

Now you shall my conscience calm,
Which, against my will, for vengeance screams
  out,
Yes, your faithfulness will fill it,
Because to me your word offers hope.
When Christians believe in you,
No enemy in all eternity
will steal them from your hands.

7. Chorale: Herr, ich glaube

Herr, ich glaube, hilf mir Schwachen,	Lord, I believe, help me, a weakling,
laß mich ja verzagen nicht;	let me falter not;
du, du kannst mich stärker machen,	thou, thou canst me stronger make,
wenn mich Sünd und Tod anficht.	when sin and death assault me.
Deiner Güte will ich trauen,	Your goodness will I trust,
bis ich fröhlich werde schauen	until I gladly see
dich, Herr Jesu, nach dem Streit	you, Lord Jesus, after the battle
in der süßen Ewigkeit.	in sweet eternity

The opening movement is a *tour-de-force* of Baroque compositional techniques, incorporating an ostinato bass into a large-scale ritornello structure, with a chorale superimposed onto choral writing that is typical of a motet. The ostinato passage in the first movement is the four-measure figure in the bass line at the opening of the work that descends by half-steps from G to D. This descending chromatic fourth, known as the *passus duriusculus* ("painful passage"), had long been associated with moments of anguish. Purcell used it in Dido's lament at the end of *Dido and Aeneas,* and Bach himself would later use it in the Credo of his B-Minor Mass for the passage that speaks of Christ's crucifixion. Here it alerts listeners even before a word is sung that the opening movement of this cantata deals with pain and suffering.

The ostinato is stated twice in the bass (m. 1–5 and 5–9) and then migrates to other voices: the first oboe (m. 9–12), second oboe (13–16), and then finally to the singers themselves, who enter in imitation (m. 17ff.). The descending line is then inverted (m. 25ff.) at the first suggestion of hope in the text ("has through your bitter death…"), but then reverts to its original descending pattern (m. 28ff.). The figure continues with similar permutations in almost every measure of the movement.

This first movement is also permeated with the melody of the chorale from which the cantata takes its name. The words and melody of *Jesu, der du meine Seele* would have been familiar to any of the parishioners hearing the first performance of this cantata. The melody falls into distinct phrases and is always presented by the soprano (beginning in m. 21). Thus, the chorale melody presents a kind of superstructure above the ostinato figure. The movement opens with an extended passage for the orchestra alone, with a dotted-rhythm melody running above the ostinato in the bass. The rhythm of this triple-meter melody is reminiscent of the sarabande, a dance common to many instrumental suites. This material functions as a ritornello throughout the entire movement, returning between the successive entrances of the chorus, as shown in the following table:

The ritornello structure of Bach, *Jesu, der du meine Seele,* BWV 78, first movement.

Section	Rit.1	Chorus 1	Rit.2	Ch.2	Rit.3	Ch.3	Rit.4	Ch.4
Measure	1	17	37	49	69	73	85	89
Tonality	g				d		F	

Section	Rit. 5	Ch.5	Rit. 6	Ch. 6	Rit. 7
Measure	99	107	122	129	140
Tonality	B♭	→ g			g (G)

Finally, by dividing the text into six distinct sections, each with its own thematic material, and each with its own set of points of imitation, Bach in effect employs the structure of the motet for the choral portions of the opening movement.

The second-movement duet is a masterpiece of word-painting. The principal thematic idea takes its cue from the text itself ("We hasten with weak, yet eager steps, / oh Jesus, oh Master, for help toward thee"). Bach sets this text to an energetic, upward-moving line that keeps falling back on itself, only to strive ever higher to a constant rhythm of steady eighth notes. The image of "weak, yet eager steps" could scarcely be captured more vividly. The two voices in turn strive with each other to reach their highest pitch.

Formally, Bach constructs this duet as a *da capo* aria:

	Section	Measure nos.	Harmony
A	Ritornello 1	1–8	B♭ major
	Solo 2	9–42	B♭ major
	Ritornello 2	43–50	B♭ major
B	Solo 2	51–60	G minor → C minor
	Ritornello 3	61–64	C minor
	Solo 3	65–80	C minor → D minor
	Ritornello 4	81–82	D minor → F major
	Solo 4	83–98	F major (=V/B♭), ("A" section *da capo*)

The subsequent recitative and aria for tenor (omitted here for reasons of space) and for bass are also full of word-painting. In the bass recitative in the fifth movement, for example, the words *Wunden* ("wounds"), *Nägel* ("nails") and *Kron* ("crown") are set to pointed dissonances; on *Grab* ("grave"), the singer descends to a deep voice register; and the strings present an agitated sixteenth note figure to emphasize the word *erschreckliches* ("terrifying") in m. 8–9. The bass aria is a duet between the vocalist and the oboist. This kind of writing for voice and solo instrument occurs frequently in Bach's music. The cantata concludes with a harmonized setting of the chorale melody *Jesu, der du meine Seele,* which had provided the cantus firmus for the opening movement, rounding out the whole to provide a sense of cyclical symmetry.

8:35 Veloce

260 ■ No. 89 Leonarda: Sonata duodecima

90 Arcangelo Corelli (1653–1713):
Concerto grosso in F Major,
Op. 6, No. 2 (ca. 1685?)

Listen
CD6   Track 1
mysearchlab
Book p. 267

Like the cantata, the term *sonata* (Italian for "that which is sounded") was something of a catchall for instrumental works of many kinds, including those for a large ensemble with more than one player to a part. In general, a Baroque sonata had no fixed number or order of movements. Isabella Leonarda, a nun who composed mostly religious vocal works, published one set of instrumental pieces, the *Sonate à 1. 2. 3. e 4. istromenti*, opus 16 (Bologna, 1693), the first sonatas published by a woman

The twelfth and final sonata in the set, the *Sonata duodecima* in D minor, is for solo violin and basso continuo. The piece recalls earlier Italian sonatas with its fluidity and formal freedom and its paratactic structure; the changes of tempo and meter are typical of sonatas and concertos of Corelli and others. The music, based on a background progression of D minor → F major (m. 84) → B♭ (m. 126) → D minor (m. 189), is harmonically rich, although the solo parts technical virtuosity is relatively restrained.

Performance notes: The performance here, on a cello, serves as a useful reminder that Baroque performers routinely adopted music for one instrument to another. In this instance, the music is simply transposed down an octave. This performance also reminds us that the cello was beginning to come into its own as a solo instrument toward the end of the seventeenth century.

No. 90 Corelli: Concerto grosso in F Major, Op. 6, No. 2

No. 90 Corelli: Concerto grosso in F Major, Op. 6, No. 2   ■ 263

■ No. 90 Corelli: Concerto grosso in F Major, Op. 6, No. 2

No. 90 Corelli: Concerto grosso in F Major, Op. 6, No. 2   ■   **265**

No. 90 Corelli: Concerto grosso in F Major, Op. 6, No. 2 ■ **267**

Arcangelo Corelli's concerti grossi are among the earliest works of their kind. Although not published until 1714, a year after the composer's death, at least some of these works were circulating in manuscript in Rome as early as the 1680s. Corelli's concerti grossi feature a ripieno of strings and basso continuo with a concertino (solo ensemble) typical of a trio sonata: two violins and basso continuo. The concertino part is continuous and—as the original title page indicates—can be performed with or without the ripieno forces. The ripieno part, in other words, is not essential to the structural integrity of these works. But without the ripieno, these works lack the timbral variety—the rapid back-and-forth between soloists and ensemble—that gives them their distinctive profile.

The formal structure of these concertos is fluid. The individual movements are not built around recurring themes—ritornelli—like the later concertos of Vivaldi and Bach, but instead move through a series of relatively brief sections that present contrasting thematic ideas in different keys and tempos. The second work of the set (op. 6, no. 2, in F major) falls into four movements, three of which—the first, third, and fourth—have distinct subsections. The first movement moves back and forth between a Vivace fanfare and an imitative Allegro. It also includes two slow sections—one in the middle (m. 40–51), the other at the end (m. 99–107)— each with its own distinct thematic material. The second movement is a continuous and relatively brief (57 measures) Allegro. The third movement opens with a Grave and moves to a thematically distinct Andante Largo. Harmonically, this movement begins in D minor and ends on C, the dominant of F. It leads without a break into the fourth movement, an Allegro in binary form (consisting, that is, of two repeated sections).

91 Antonio Vivaldi (1678–1741):
Concerto in A minor, Op. 3, No. 8,
first movement (1711)

No. 91 Vivaldi: Concerto in A minor, Op. 3, No. 8 ■ **273**

■ No. 91 Vivaldi: Concerto in A minor, Op. 3, No. 8

The solo and tutti parts of Vivaldi's Concerto for Two Violins, op. 3, no. 8, in A minor, are structurally interdependent: even though the two soloists often double the ripieno violins, these parts diverge at times, as at the beginning of the Solo I section in the first movement (m. 16). In a concerto by Corelli, the ripieno would have simply dropped out entirely at this point.

Thematically, the opening ritornello of Vivaldi's concerto introduces three of the work's four principal thematic ideas (see textbook, p. 269). The opening unison head motif (1) is typical of many concertos of this era: it presents a memorable, sharply profiled idea that is immediately recognizable whenever it returns over the course of the movement. The middle section of the opening ritornello (2) presents an idea that is more fluid and sequential, while the closing section of the ritornello (3), with its dominant pedal point, clearly signals the arrival of a cadence. These three ideas, taken together, form a self-contained unit consisting of a beginning (1), middle (2), and end (3). Over the course of the movement, however, Vivaldi breaks up the consitutent subunits of the ritornello, combining them with a new idea (4), first presented by the solo violins in m. 16.

In the broadest terms, then, the overall form of this movement consists of an alternation of ritornello and solo sections (see diagram, below). At a more detailed level, however, the form is more complicated than this simple description might suggest. Almost all of the solo and ritornello sections are interrupted at some point by interpolations of an opposing texture. Solo I, for example, is interrupted by a brief return of tutti texture at m. 22, with a brief restatement of the ritornello's closing idea (3). Ritornello II, in turn, is interrupted by a brief solo passage in m. 39–41. The alternation of ritornello and solo is thus more a general organizational principle than a rigid scheme.

Section	Harmonic area	Measures (number of measures)	Thematic ideas
Ritornello I	i	1–16 (16)	(1) (2) (3)
Solo I	i → III	16–36 (20)	(4) punctuated by (3)
Ritornello II	III → iv	37–47 (11)	(2)
Solo II	iv → i	48–67 (20)	(2) punctuated by (1), (3), (4)
Ritornello III	i	68–71 (4)	(1)
Solo III	i	71–78 (6)	(2) punctuated by (3)
Ritornello IV	i	79–93 (14)	(3)

François Couperin (1668–1733):
Pièces de clavecin, Book I,
Second ordre (excerpts) (1713)

((•—Listen
CD6   Tracks 3–4
mysearchlab
Book p. 273

La Prude.

Sarabande.

Premiere
Courante.

Couperin liked to place provocative, often enigmatic, titles at the head of individual dance pieces within a suite. He published four *livres* for clavecin (1713, 1717, 1722, and 1730), comprising 27 consecutively numbered *ordres,* as well as an influential treatise, *L'Art de toucher le clavecin* ("The Art of Playing the Harpsichord," 1716), which includes eight preludes and an allemande.

Like other *ordres* in the first book, the second *ordre,* in D minor, features a mixture of standard Baroque dances and programmatic character pieces; the latter would become a prominent piano genre during the 19th century (see textbook, Chapter 16). Here, the Premiere courante meets the definition of binary dance form: the first half cadences on the dominant, the second half flirts with a cadence in C Major but evades it to finish in the tonic. The Sarabande (the fourth piece in the *ordre*) has the title "La Prude"; this may refer to a specific individual, or a type, or no one in particular, but at this point we are at a loss to know precisely (although research into the meanings behind Couperin's titles continues). But, unlike Kuhnau's "Biblical" sonatas and Marais's *Le Tableau de l'opération de la taille* (see textbook, Chapter 10), this Sarabande can simply be heard as the slow triple-meter dance it is, with a half-cadence at the midpoint. In the second half, after a cadence in the relative major, there is a subtle byplay between hands as the music modulates back to D minor, a moment when the nearly constant ornamentation rests to allow the retransition to shine through.

Is the character of "La Prude" expressed through nonstop ornamentation, and should this be emphasized by the performer? On the contrary: unlike Italian keyboard music, the highly ornamented French style of the *clavecinistes* was usually written in by the composer. In Couperin's case, he insisted on it; in 1722 he complains of his "surprise, after the pains that I have taken to indicate the ornaments appropriate to my pieces … to hear people who have learnt them without heeding my instructions. Such carelessness is unpardonable, all the more as it is no arbitrary matter to put in such ornaments as one wishes."

"**Le cahos**" from
Les élémens (1737)

Listen
CD6   Track 5
mysearchlab
Book p. 275

© 1993 by Editions Salabert, Paris
International copyright secured all rights reserved
EDITIONS SALABERT S.A. 22, rue Chauchat 75009 PARIS

Tous droits réservés pour tous pays
Toute reproduction intégrale ou partielle du présent ouvrage est illicite (Loi du 11 mars 1957) et sanctionnée par le Code Pénal

Many suites in the Baroque era were programmatic—that is, they were associated with a particular extramusical idea, person, or event. Among the most extraordinary of all instrumental suites is Jean-Féry Rebel's *Les élémens* ("The Elements"). The first movement, "Chaos," begins with a chord that strikes even 21st-century ears as chaotic. It is a simultaneous sounding of all the notes in a D-minor scale (D-E-F-G-A-B♭-C♯) with the remarkable figuration in the basso continuo of

♯7
♭6
5
4
3
2

over a low D. The beginning of the first movement, Rebel noted in his preface to the score, "represents the confusion that prevails among the elements before that moment in which, subject to invariable laws, they assume the place prescribed for them by the order of Nature." The bass, he goes on to explain, "expresses the Earth through the tied notes, played percussively. The flutes, with their rising and falling lines, imitate the flow and murmuring of water. The air is depicted by long-held notes followed by cadences in the piccolos. And finally, the violins represent the active nature of fire through their vigorous and brilliant strokes . . . I have dared to connect the idea of the confusion of the elements with a confusion of harmony . . . These notes proceed to a unison in a progression that is natural, and after a dissonance, we hear a perfect chord [i.e., a unison]."

94 Girolamo Frescobaldi
(1583–1643): **Toccata IX** from
Il Secondo Libro di Toccate (1627)

Listen
CD6   Track 6
mysearchlab
Book p. 276

*) sic: cf. app. crit.

Non senza fatiga si giunge al fine

No. 94 Frescobaldi: Toccata IX ■ 295

The Ninth Toccata from Frescobaldi's *Second Book of Toccatas,* although unusually intricate, is nonetheless representative of the genre as a whole. Rapid passagework combined with freedom of form had long been characteristic of the toccata. Highly episodic, Frescobaldi's toccata moves rapidly through a variety of textures, registers, rhythms, and meters. Some sections last only a few measures. The rhythms are constantly shifting and at times quite intricate (for example, m. 11, 22, 25); the right and left hands occasionally work in cross rhythms (m. 56–60, 65); and the passagework, which is distinctly idiomatic to the harpsichord (as opposed to the organ), is dazzling at times (m. 25–26, 50–54). Small wonder, then, that Frescobaldi should add the remark at the very end of this work: *Non senza fatiga si giunge al fine* ("Not without effort does one arrive at the end").

95   Dietrich Buxtehude (1637–1707):
Praeludium in G minor,
BuxWV 149 (ca. 1675–1689)

((•─Listen

CD6   Track 7
mysearchlab
Book p. 276

Dietrich Buxtehude's Praeludium in G minor for organ (BuxWV 149), written sometime between 1675 and 1689, consists of a series of discrete sections, each with its own distinctive theme and texture. The long imitative sections are typical of the prelude and many other free keyboard genres in the 17th century. Buxtehude's Praeludium ends with an extended rhapsody that sounds almost improvisational.

THE STRUCTURE OF BUXTEHUDE'S PRAELUDIUM IN G MINOR, BUX WV 149.		
Measures	Indicated tempo	Texture
1–20	None	Passagework in hands; ostinato figure in pedals
21–56	Alla breve	Imitative
57–79	Allegro	Free, running bass against chords
80–140	Largo	Imitative, triple meter
141–61	Largo	Free, quasi improvisatory

Buxtehude's Praeludium exhibits three different kinds of virtuosity:

- compositional, reflected in the wide range of techniques the composer deploys, from rapid passagework to strict polyphonic imitation;
- performative, as reflected in the extreme technical demands of the writing;
- instrumentational, as reflected in the way it calls on almost all the resources of the organ, from shifts in register to demanding pedalwork.

96 J. S. Bach: **The Well-Tempered Clavier,** Book I (excerpts) (1722)

Listen
CD6 Track 8
mysearchlab
Book p. 278

Prelude and Fugue No. 1 in C Major, BWV 846

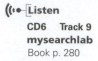

CD6 Track 9
mysearchlab
Book p. 280

Prelude and Fugue No. 4 in C# minor, BWV 848

a 5.

The two books of Bach's *Well-Tempered Clavier* present a rich variety of imitative and nonimitative keyboard pieces. Each book consists of a series of 24 paired preludes and fugues, with one pair in each of the 24 major and minor keys. No one is exactly certain what the "Well-Tempered" of the title means. Some believe it reflects Bach's advocacy of equal temperament, a system of tuning that allowed keyboard players to play in any key (see Focus: "Systems of Temperament"). Others maintain that "Well-Tempered" is a vague term that leaves much to the discretion of the performer to use whatever tuning system is appropriate to the work at hand. Bach's purpose in writing the *Well-Tempered Clavier,* according to this line of thought, was to demonstrate the feasability of writing and performing works in all 24 keys, leaving the question of tuning to the performer. There were many systems of temperament at the time that could accommodate a wide variety of keys reasonably well, even if Bach's contemporaries disagreed on the precise limitations of reasonableness. Much depended on a performer's willingness to tolerate certain imperfections of certain intervals in certain keys.

In any event, Bach organized each book of the *Well-Tempered Clavier* according to the ascending chromatic scale, with major-mode works in each key followed by a corresponding work in the minor mode:

Prelude and Fugue in C major
Prelude and Fugue in C minor
Prelude and Fugue in C♯ major
Prelude and Fugue in C♯ minor
Prelude and Fugue in D major
Prelude and Fugue in D minor
Prelude and Fugue in E♭ major
Prelude and Fugue in E♭ minor
Prelude and Fugue in E major
Prelude and Fugue in E minor

and so on.

Reflecting Bach's passion for exploring the many possibilities of a self-imposed limitation, all the preludes and fugues are different from one another. The C-major Prelude follows a pattern of broken chords in a manner known as style brisée ("broken style"), adopted from the arpeggiated ("broken") chords and figures typically found in lute music. Not coincidentally, this piece remains a favorite among guitar players. The Prelude in C# minor is in the style of a sarabande, a slow dance in triple meter. Some analysts have discerned subtle thematic or motivic links between certain preludes and their associated fugues, but in general these, too, are musically independent of each other.

By the same token, there is no standard pattern for the fugues. Some of them—especially the longer ones—have more than one subject, and these do not necessarily all appear at the outset. A new subject enters the Fugue in C# minor of Bach's *Well-Tempered Clavier,* Book I, for example, in m. 36, still another in m. 49.

97 Johann Pachelbel (1652–1706):
Chorale prelude on the **Magnificat peregrini toni** (late 17th century)

((•—Listen
CD6 Track 10
mysearchlab
Book p. 280

Chorale preludes were written to serve as instrumental introductions to the congregational singing of a chorale in church. Given this function, these works tend to be brief and relatively straightforward. Johann Pachelbel's chorale prelude *Magnificat peregrini toni* is typical of the genre. The chorale melody had been adopted from the Ninth Psalm Tone of the Roman Catholic liturgy (the *tonus peregrinus* or "pilgrim tone," so called because it moves from one recitation tone in its first half to a different one in its second). In Protestant services, this melody was commonly associated with the Magnificat, the words uttered by the Virgin Mary when she learns from the annunciating angel that she is to bear the Christ child ("My soul doth magnify the Lord," Luke 1: 47–55). In Pachelbel's setting the tune is stated in its entirety in long notes in the upper voice, with the other voices weaving around it. The two measures of introduction present a brief point of imitation on the opening of the theme; once the melody enters in m. 3, the two lower voices engage in antiphonal passagework that is flowing but unspectacular: the focus of attention here, after all, is on the melody in the upper voice. The middle voice again introduces a brief point of imitation in m. 9, anticipating the first notes of the second phrase of the chorale melody while the upper voice pauses between the phrases. But once again, the imitation soon breaks off. The rhythmic acceleration in m. 12–13 provides variety, and the whole concludes with a *tièrce de picardie* (picardy third)—a major third at the end of a work otherwise in minor mode—in m. 19. Such endings had become commonplace for works in the minor mode by 1700. Evidence suggests that even if a sharpened third was not explicitly notated on the final cadence in a score, performers were expected to provide it—a late vestige of musica ficta.

98 J. S. Bach: Chorale prelude on
Meine Seele erhebt den Herren,
BWV 648 (1748)

((•—Listen
CD6 Tracks 12–21
mysearchlab
Book p. 284

Johann Sebastian Bach's chorale prelude on the same melody as Pachelbel's *Magnificat peregrini toni* exhibits a very different approach to the genre. Originally part of his cantata BWV 10 (1724), later rearranged for organ (published 1748), this work also places the melody in an upper voice in long note values. The two measures of introduction in Pachelbel's version are replaced here by an eight-measure fugal exposition on a chromatic theme unrelated to the chorale. Once the chorale melody enters (m. 9), the imitation in the lower voices continues. The brief pause within the chorale melody—a single measure's rest in Pachelbel's version—expands here to eight full measures, once again on the independent chromatic motive. Even after the chorale melody concludes, we hear an additional seven measures of imitation, with the piece ending as it had begun, a statement of the chromatic subject in the pedals.

The effect of all this is strangely haunting. The chorale melody has metamorphosed into a transparent alto line (played by the right hand!) into which Bach fits a powerful piece showing his incomparable contrapuntal and pedaling skills. We can, however, sympathize with the reaction of many of his contemporaries, who found such preludes disconcerting. Early in his career Bach was called to task for the way in which he harmonized chorales being sung by parishioners. According to the letter of reprimand, Bach had "made many curious *variationes* in the chorale, and mingled many strange tones in it, and … the Congregation has been confused by it."

Variatio 4. a 1 Clav.

Measure	1–8		9–16	
Theme	‖:G-F♯-E-D-B-C-D-G		G-F♯-E-A-F♯-G-A-D:‖	
Tonality	I	I	I	V

Measure	17–24		25–32	
Theme	‖:D-B-C-B-G-A-B-E		C-B-A-D-G-C-D-G:‖	
Tonality	V	vi	ii^6	I

Johann Sebastian Bach's "Goldberg" Variations offer perhaps the most spectacular example in the entire history of music of the elaborations possible within the framework of a simple bass line. For many years, it was believed that Bach wrote this set of harpsichord variations on behalf of one of his pupils, Johann Gottlieb Goldberg, who in turn was employed by a certain Baron von Keyserlingk. Legend has it that the Baron had trouble getting to sleep at night and that these variations were designed to help him while away the evening hours. But the story is demonstrably false, because Goldberg was only about 14 years old when Bach wrote this work.

The "Goldberg" Variations, like the *Well-Tempered Clavier* and the late, unfinished *Art of the Fugue,* exemplifies Bach's passion for writing encyclopedic works. In the *Well-Tempered Clavier* he explored the permutations of free preludes and imitative fugues in every possible key. In the *Art of the Fugue* he would explore various ways in which different fugal devices can be brought to bear on a single subject. In the "Goldberg" Variations he systematically explored the technique of both variation and canon.

The variations take us through an astonishing set of permutations on a single idea. The source of that idea is elusive. Bach's use of the term "aria" to designate the opening variation draws our attention to the soprano line, but the theme, spelled out here, is actually in the bass:

Bach further concealed the theme with added notes, even on its first presentation in the aria. In the first reprise, the theme's pitches mostly coincide with the longer notes on the downbeats in the bass line (predominantly half notes and dotted half notes); in the second reprise, the notes of the theme do not coincide with the downbeat nearly as often.

Bach uses this bass progression as the foundation for all subsequent variations. In Variation 1, for example, the theme is readily apparent on the downbeat of every measure in the first reprise, but harder to follow in the second reprise.

Another structural device Bach uses throughout this set is a series of canons. Every third variation (Numbers 3, 6, 9, 12, etc.) presents a canon in the two upper voices, creating a trio-sonata texture with two high voices and a bass. The bass line operates independently of the canon, though always providing the necessary notes of the theme in the proper order. Each canon, moreover, is written at an interval one step greater than the one before. Thus, the first canon (Variation 3) is at the unison: the second voice enters one measure after the first, but at the same pitch. The second canon is composed at the interval of a second (no easy task), with the second voice entering one whole step above the first and a measure behind. The third canon is a canon at the third, and so on.

In a third level of complexity, Bach incorporates a variety of musical styles within the "Goldberg" Variations. Variation 16, for example, which opens the unlabeled second part of the work, is in the style of a French overture. Number 10 is a fugue. Number 7 is a gigue. In addition, the work contains many dazzling passages, as in Variation 14, that require a virtuoso to perform.

Performance notes: Like the organ, the more sophisticated harpsichords of Bach's era included multiple stops, settings that could alter the sound of the instrument's tone. The dual manual harpsichords of the day even featured a second keyboard; by setting the stops in advance, a player could thereby alter the tone of the instrument quite rapidly simply by moving from one keyboard to the other. The dual manual harpsichord also helps the performer avoid some serious problems of hand-crossing that can occur in this particular work for any musician who performs it on a single-manual instrument like the piano.

Two recordings of the theme and first four variations of this work are presented here: by Gustav Leonhardt, on a harpsichord (tracks 12–16); and by Glenn Gould, on a modern-day grand piano (tracks 17–21). Gould's performance is discussed in detail in the textbook on p. 286.

CREDITS

Cover: "Toccata IX," by Girolama Frescobaldi, from *Il Secondo Libro di Toccate*, published in 1637.

1. Apollo's Lyre: *Greek Music and Music Theory in Antiquity and the Middle Ages* by Thomas J. Mathiesen. Copyright © 1999 by Thomas J. Mathiesen. Reprinted by permission.

2. Plainchant, Mass for Christmas Day.

3. Plainchant, Vespers on Pentecost Tuesday. *Antiphon Pacem relinquo vobis and Psalm 116 Laudate Dominum.*

4. Plainchant, Hymn *Pange lingua gloriosi corporis mysterium.*

5. "Ordo Virtutum" by Hildegard von Bingen. Copyright © 2013 by Hildegard Publishing Company. Used by permission of Theodore Presser/Carl Fischer, LLC.

6. "A chantar" by Beatriz de Dia, translated by Hendrick van der Werf, from THE EXTANT TROUBADOUR MELODIES, by Hendrick van der Werf. Copyright © 1984 by Hendrick van der Werf. Used by permission of the author.

7. "Baron (Baros), de mon dan covet" by Peire Vidal, translated by Hendrick van der Werf, from THE EXTANT TROUBADOUR MELODIES, by Hendrick van der Werf. Copyright © 1984 by Hendrick van der Werf. Used by permission of the author.

8. Cantigas de Santa Maria, no. 140: *A Santa Maria dadas*. Reprinted with permission of the publisher from Martin Cunningham, ed., *Alfonso X El Sabio, Cantigas de Loor* (Dublin: University College Dublin Press, 2000).

9. Walther von der Vogelweide, *Palästinalied.*

10. Kyrie *Cunctipotens genitor deus*. Codex Calistinus, Cathedral of Santiago de Compostela, f. 190. New edition by Mark Evan Bonds from the Codex Calixtinus, f. 190r. Additional text from *Analecta hymnica medii aevi*, ed. Clemens Blume and Guido M. Drewes, vol. 47, *Tropi gradualis* (Leipzig: O. R. Reisland, 1905), p. 50. New edition by Samuel Brannon based on manuscript sources from the 16th century.

11. "Leonin, 'Viderunt Omnes,' 2-vv. organum" from pages 63–68 of *Le Magnus Liber Organi de Notre-Dame de Paris*, vol. 7: *Les Organa et les Clausules a Deux Voix du Manuscrit de Wolfenbuttel, Herzog August Bibliothek, Cod. Guelf. 628 Helmst*. Ed.Edward H. Roesner (Monaco: Editions de l'Oiseau-Lyre, Copyright © 2009).

12. "Pérotin, 'Viderunt Omnes,' 4-vv. organum." From pages 1–14 of *Le Magnus Liber Organi de Notre-Dame de Paris*, vol. 1: *Les Quadrupla et Triple de Paris* (Monaco: Editions de l'Oiseau-Lyre, Copyright © 1993).

13. "Leonin, 'Viderunt Omnes,' 2-vv. organum." From page 17 of *Le Magnus Liber Organi de Notre-Dame De Paris*, vol. 5: *Les Organa et les Clausules a Deux Voix... Florence 29.1*, FASC. 5 Ed. Rebecca Baltzer (Monaco: Editions de l'Oiseau-Lyre, Copyright © 1995).

14. *The Earliest Motets* edited by Hans Tischler. Copyright © 1982 Yale University Press. Reprinted by permission.

15. "Motet Super te/ Sed fulsit/ Dominus. Four voices." From pages 170 of *English Music of the Thirteenth and Early Fourteenth Centuries*. Ed. Ernest H. Sanders. Polyphonic Music of the Fourteenth Century 14 (Monaco: Editions de l'Oiseau-Lyre, Copyright © 1993).

16. Motet *A Paris/On parole/Frese nouvelle*, pp. 189–90 in *The Montpellier Codex*, Part 3: *Fascicles 6, 7, and 8*, edited by Hans Tischler. *Recent Researches in the Music of the Middle Ages and Early Renaissance*, vol. 6 & 7. Madison, WI: A-R Editions, Inc., 1978. English translation of text by Alfonso d'Avalos from *The European Musical Heritage, 800–1750* [compiled by Sarah Fuller]; consulting editor in music, Alan W. Schindler, 1/e. NY: Knopf, © 1987. By permission of The McGraw-Hill Companies.

17. *Music in Medieval Europe* by Jeremy Yudkin. Copyright © 1989 Jeremy Yudkin. Reprinted by permission. Conductus, *Flos ut rosa floruit*. London: British Library, add. 27630. *Music in Medieval Europe*, 1st edition. © 1989 Text and translation reprinted from Jeremy Yudkin.

18. Philippe de Vitry (?), *Garrit Gallus / In nova fert / Neuma* from *Roman de Fauvel*. Text and translation from *Anthology of Medieval Music* edited by Richard Hoppin. Copyright © 1978 by W.W. Norton & Company. Used by permission of W.W. Norton & Company, Inc.

19. Guillaume de Machaut, La Messe de Nostre Dame (Kyrie). Reprinted with permission from Leo Schrade, ed. Guillaume de Machaut. Oeurves completes, vol. 3; La Messe de Nostre-Dame (Monaco: Editions de L'Oiseau-Lyre, 1977).

20. Guillaume de Machaut, *Je puis trop bien ma dame comparer*. From Leo Schrade, ed. Guillaume de Machaut, Oeuvres completes, vol. 4; Les Ballades, Les Virelais (Monaco: Editions de l'Oiseau-Lyre, 1977).

21. Guillaume de Machaut, *Douce dame jolie*. From Leo Schrade, ed. Guillaume de Machaut, Oeurves completes, vol. 4; Les Ballades, Les Virelais (Monaco: Editions de l'Oiseau-Lyre, 1977).

22. Guillaume de Machaut, *Ma fin est mon commencement*.

23. Excerpt from pages 161–164 of *French Secular Music: Manuscript Chantilly, Musee Conde 564; Polyphonic Music of the 14th Century*, vol. 18 by Gordon J. Greene, ed. (Monaco: Editions de l'Oiseau Lyre. Copyright © 1981). English translation by Rebecca Dixon. Copyright © 2003 by Rebecca Dixon. Used by permission.

24. Francesco Landini, Complete Works, vol. 1: Two-Part Ballate. Copyright © 1982 by Editions l'Oiseau Lyre. English translation by Giovanni Carsaniga from I am Music: Works by Francesco Landini, Copyright © 1997 by Move Records, Carlton, South Australia. Used by permission.

25. Jacopo da Bologna, *Non al suo amante*. English translation from *The European Musical Heritage: 800–1750* [compiled by] Sarah Fuller; consulting editor in music, Allan W. Schinder. 1/e. NY: Knopf © 1987. By permission of the McGraw-Hill Companies.

26. Lorenzo da Firenze, *A poste messe*. In Nino Pirrotta, ed., *The Music of Fourteenth-Century Italy,* vol. 3: Corpus mensurabilis musicae, 8-3 (American Institute of Musicology, 1962). Reprinted with permission. English translation courtesy of Vanguard Classics, © 1971, 1974.

27. Johannes Ciconia, *Doctorum principem/Melodia suavissma/Vir mitis*. Text and translation from Margaret Bent and Anne Hallmark, ed. *The Works of Johannes Ciconia* (Monaco: Editions de l'Oiseau-Lyre, 1982).

28. Anonymous, *Sumer is icumen in*. From *A Cappella: An Anthology of Unaccompanied Choral music from seven centuries*. Compiled and edited by John Gardner and Simon Harris. © Oxford University Press 1992. Used by permission. All rights reserved.

29. "Edi be thu, heven-queene." English translation from *Medieval English Lyrics* by E.J. Dobson and F. Harrison. Copyright © 1979 David Higham Associates. Reprinted by permission.

30. *Medieval Instrumental Dances* edited by Timothy McGee. Copyright © 1989 Indiana University Press. Reprinted by permission of Indiana University Press.

31. John Dunstable, *Quam pulchra es*.

32. Du Fay, *Conditor alme siderum*.

33. Du Fay, *Nuper rosarum flores*. English translations from *Norton Anthology of Western Music,* Vol. 1, edited by Claude V. Palisca. NY: W.W. Norton & Company, Inc.

34. Josquin des Prez, *Ave Maria . . . virgo serena*. English translation MEB.

35. Du Fay, *Se la face ay pale*. English translation MEB.

36. Du Fay, Kyrie and Gloria from *Missa se la face ay pale*. In Heinrich Besseler, ed., *Guillaume du Fay, Opera Omnia*, Corpus mensurabilis musicae, 1-3 (American Institute of Musicology, Middleton, Wisc., 1962). Reprinted with permission.

37. *Missa Prolationem* by Johannes Ockeghem; Edited by David Condon. © Fazer Music Inc., Helsinki 1992 (In Fazer Editions of Early Music). Printed by permission of Fennica Gehrman Oy, Helsinki. Reprinted by permission.

38. "*Fortuna Desperata: Thirty-Six Settings Of An Italian Song*," from *Recent Researches in the Music of the Middle Ages and Early Renaissance*, vol. 37, edited by Honey Meconi. Copyright © 2001 A-R Editions, Inc. Reprinted by permission. Antoine Busnois (?), Fortuna desperata. Text and translation from pp. 3–4 in Fortuna Desperata: Thirty-Six Settings of an Italian Song, edited by Honey Meconi, *Recent Researches in the Music of the Middle Ages and Early Renaissance*, vol. 37. (Madison, WI: A-R Editions, Inc., 2001).

39. Josquin *Missa Fortuna desperata*, (Kyrie and Agnus Die). Reprinted from *Werken van Josquin des Prez*, Missen, Ser. 3, Deel 1 (Amsterdam: G. Alsbach, 1929).

40. Josquin, *Kyrie* from *Missa pange lingua*.

41. "Absalon, fili mi" by Josquin des Prez, from THE NEW JOSQUIN EDITION UTRECHT. Copyright © 2002 by Koninklijke Vereniging voor Nederlandse Muziekgeschiedenis. Used by permission. Available for purchase at www.kvnm.nl

42. Du Fay Chansons, translation by Keith Anderson. Copyright © Naxos of America. Reprinted by permission.

43. *The Mellon Chansonnier* edited by Leeman Perkins and Howard Garey. Copyright © 1979 Yale University Press. Reprinted by permission.

44. Heinrich Isaac, *Innsbruck, ich muss dich lassen*. Denkmaler des Tonkunst in Osterreich, Vol. 28 (publ. 1907) edited by Rafael Ornes. Copyright © 1999 by the Choral Public Domain Library (http://www.cpdl.org) Edition may be freely distributed, duplicated, performed or recorded.

45. "Hor venduto ho la speranza" by Marchetto Cara, translated by Peggy Forsyth.

70. Giulio Caccini, *Sfogava con le stelle*. Text and translation reprinted with permission of the publisher from H. Wiley Hitchcock, ed., Giulio Caccini, Le nuovo musiche, Recent Researches in the Music of the Baroque Era, vol. 9. (Madison, WI: A-R Editions, Inc., 1970).

71. Monteverdi *Cruda Amarilli* from *Madrigals,* Book Five. English translation MEB.

72. Monteverdi, *T'amo mia vita* from *Madrigals,* Book Five. From Sylvia Glickman (Editor), Martha Furman Schleifer (Editor). Women Composers, Music Through the Ages, 1E. © 2006 Gale, a part of Cengage Learning, Inc. Reproduced by permission. www.cengage.com/permissions

73. *Tutte le Opera* by Claudio Monteverdi vol. 9, edited by G.F. Malipiero. Copyright © 1929 by Universal Edition. Reprinted with kind permission by Universal Edition A.G. Wien/UE 32144.

74. "Lasciatemi qui solo" - Modern edition and English translation © Suzanne G. Cusick.

75. TRADIMENTO! by Barbara Strozzi. English translation by Carol Plantamura. Copyright © 1985 Leonarda Productions, Inc. www.leonarda.com.

76. "Enfin la beauté que j'adore" by Etienne Mouline, translated by Ellen Hargis. Reprinted with permission.

77. Monteverdi, *Orfeo: Favola in Musica,* excerpt from Act II from *Tutte le opera di Claudio Monteverdi,* edited by G. F. Malipiero. © 1929 by Universal Edition © renewed. All rights reserved. Used by permission of European American Music Distributors, LLC, U.S. and Canadian agent for Universal Edition. English translation by Robert Stuart, Chester © 1923. 1934 (renewed), J. & W. Chester Ltd. By permission of G. Schirmer, Inc. & Associated Music Publishers, Inc., a division of Music Sales Corporation. International copyright secured. All rights reserved. Reprinted by permission.

78. Monteverdi, *L'incoronazione di Poppea,* Act I, Scene 3. Libretto by Giovanni Busenello. Edited by Alan Curtis. Copyright © 1989 Novello & Company Limited. International copyright secured. All rights reserved. Reprinted by permission of G. Schirmer, Inc. (ASCAP).

79. "Singet dem Herren ein neues Lied" from *Neue Ausgabe Samtlicher Werke* by Heinrich Schütz, edited by Werner Bittinger. Copyright © 1964 Bärenreiter-Verlag KarlVötterle GmbH & Co. KG, Kassel. Reprinted by permission.

80. Schütz, *Saul, was verfolgst du mich.* Reprinted with permission of Carus-Verlag Stuttgart GmbH, Sielminger Str. 51, D-70771 Leinfelden-Echterdingen, Germany; from Stuttgarter Schützausgabe, ed. G. Graulich, English text by Derek McCulloch. © 1969 by Hanssler Verlag, Neuhausen-Stuttgart.

81. Jean-Baptiste Lully, *Armide,* Act II, Overture and Scene 5 Lully, *Oeurvres completes,* serie III, vol. 14; Hildesheim: G. Olms, 2003.

82. "Giulio Cesare: Act I (exc), scenes 5-7" by Georg Friedrich Handel. English translation by James D. Wootton Copyright © 2005 Harmonia Mundi S.A. Reprinted by permission.

83. Henry Purcell, *Dido and Aeneas,* Act I, Scene I (excerpt).

84. John Gay and Johann Christoph Pepusch, *The Beggar's Opera* (excerpts). From *The Music of John Gay's The Beggar's Opera.* Edited and arranged by Jeremy Barlow. © Oxford University Press 1990. Used by permission. All rights reserved.

85. Giacomo Carissimi, *Jephte* (excerpt). Edited by Janet Beat. Copyright © 1974 by Novello & Company Limited. International copyright secured. All rights reserved. Reprinted with permission of G. Schirmer, Inc. (ASCAP).

86. Handel, *Zadok the Priest.*

87. Elisabeth Jacquet de la Geurre, *Judith, "Le coup est achevé".* From Elisabeth-Claude Jacquet de la Guerre: Collected Works. Edited by Mary Cyr Volume 3: Sacred Vocal Works. New York: Broude Trust, 2005. Translation from CD booklet V700020 Pierre Verany.

88. Johann Sebastian Bach. *Neue Ausgabe Sämtlicher Werke, Kantataen Zum 13 Und 14 Nach Trinitatis, Serie I: Kantaten, B and 21.* Edited by Werner Neumann, BA 5013. Copyright © 1953 Baerenreiter-Verlag. Reprinted by permission of the publisher.

89. Isabella Leonarda, "Sonata duodecima," pp. 261–265 in Isabella Leonarda: Twelve Sonatas Opus 16, edited by Stewart Carter, Recent Researches in the Music of the Baroque Era, vol. 113. Middleton, WI: A-R Editions, Inc., 2001.

90. Arcangelo Corelli, Concerto grosso, Op. 6, No. 2

91. Antonio Vivaldi, Concerto in A minor, Op. 3, No. 8, first movement. Copyright © 1965 by G. Ricordi & E. Editori, Milano. All rights reserved. Reprinted by permission.

92. François Couperin, *Pièces de clavecin,* Book I, Second ordre, Premiere Courante and La Prude (Sarabande). From Couperin: Pièces de clavecin, Livre I. Paris, 1716–17. Edited by J. Brahms and F. Chrysander.

93. Jean-Féry Rebel, *Les élémens:* first movement, ("Le cahos"). Reprinted with permission from edition by Catherine Cessac (Paris: Editions Salabert, 1993).

94. *Opere Complete,* Vol. 3: *Il Secondo Libro di Toccate* by Girolamo Frescobaldi, edited by Etienne Darbellay. Copyright © 1979 Edizioni Suvini Zerboni—Sugar Music S.P.A., Milan. Reprinted by permission.

95. Dietrich Buxtehude, Praeludium in G minor, BuxWV 149.

96. J. S. Bach, *The Well-Tempered Clavier,* Book I, excerpts.

97. Johann Pachelbel, Chorale prelude on the *Magnificat peregrini toni*.

98. J. S. Bach, Chorale prelude on *Meine Seele erhebt den Herren,* BWV 648, from *Sechs Choräle von verschiedener Art* (the "Schübler" chorales).

99. J. S. Bach, *"Goldberg" Variations* (excerpt).